CAMBRIDGE LIBRARY COLLECTION

Books of enduring scholarly value

Literary Studies

This series provides a high-quality selection of early printings of literary works, textual editions, anthologies and literary criticism which are of lasting scholarly interest. Ranging from Old English to Shakespeare to early twentieth-century work from around the world, these books offer a valuable resource for scholars in reception history, textual editing, and literary studies.

The Catalogue of the Library of the Wisbech Museum

Wisbech in north Cambridgeshire was a wealthy port in the eighteenth and nineteenth centuries, and was home to bankers, writers and influential social reformers including Thomas Clarkson. Its museum, founded in 1847, contains about six thousand books bequeathed by Chauncy Hare Townshend (1798–1868), a friend of Charles Dickens who shared Dickens' fascination with mesmerism and the occult. His library was typical of 'a gentleman of wealth and great culture' and contained works of fiction in several languages, non-fiction and science, many of which were rare and finely bound. Since 1877 the Museum has also housed the library of the Wisbech Literary Society (founded in 1781), which focused on history, biography and travel. This 1882 catalogue of the 12,000 volumes in the two Wisbech collections provides fascinating insights into the reading habits of a successful British business community on the one hand, and an influential Victorian collector on the other.

AF 148406

Cambridge University Press has long been a pioneer in the reissuing of out-of-print titles from its own backlist, producing digital reprints of books that are still sought after by scholars and students but could not be reprinted economically using traditional technology. The Cambridge Library Collection extends this activity to a wider range of books which are still of importance to researchers and professionals, either for the source material they contain, or as landmarks in the history of their academic discipline.

Drawing from the world-renowned collections in the Cambridge University Library, and guided by the advice of experts in each subject area, Cambridge University Press is using state-of-the-art scanning machines in its own Printing House to capture the content of each book selected for inclusion. The files are processed to give a consistently clear, crisp image, and the books finished to the high quality standard for which the Press is recognised around the world. The latest print-on-demand technology ensures that the books will remain available indefinitely, and that orders for single or multiple copies can quickly be supplied.

The Cambridge Library Collection will bring back to life books of enduring scholarly value (including out-of-copyright works originally issued by other publishers) across a wide range of disciplines in the humanities and social sciences and in science and technology.

The Catalogue of the Library of the Wisbech Museum

Comprising the Books Formerly Belonging to the Wisbech Literary Society, and Those of the Townshend Bequest

Anonymous

CAMBRIDGE UNIVERSITY PRESS

Cambridge, New York, Melbourne, Madrid, Cape Town,
Singapore, São Paolo, Delhi, Tokyo, Mexico City

Published in the United States of America by Cambridge University Press, New York

www.cambridge.org
Information on this title: www.cambridge.org/9781108031189

© in this compilation Cambridge University Press 2011

This edition first published 1882
This digitally printed version 2011

ISBN 978-1-108-03118-9 Paperback

This book reproduces the text of the original edition. The content and language reflect
the beliefs, practices and terminology of their time, and have not been updated.

Cambridge University Press wishes to make clear that the book, unless originally published
by Cambridge, is not being republished by, in association or collaboration with, or
with the endorsement or approval of, the original publisher or its successors in title.

THE

CATALOGUE OF THE LIBRARY

OF THE

WISBECH MUSEUM,

COMPRISING THE BOOKS FORMERLY BELONGING TO

THE WISBECH LITERARY SOCIETY,

AND THOSE OF THE

TOWNSHEND BEQUEST.

———————

WISBECH :

PRINTED BY LEACH AND SON, HIGH STREET.

1882.

PREFACE.

TWO entirely distinct collections of Books are repre-
sented in this Catalogue. The first is the Library
of the Literary Society, established in the town in 1781,
and by the munificence of the President, Mr. Peckover,
and others, transferred to the Wisbech Museum in 1877.
The second consists of the books of the Townshend bequest,
acquired by the Museum Trustees in 1868. Each collection
has its own special character. The Literary Society's
books have been slowly accumulated during its century of
existence, and the taste of the different generations of
readers is displayed in the subjects selected. Works of
History, Biography, and of Travel are very much more
abundant than those of Fiction, or the Drama. Theological
and political literature has been designedly, for the most
part, excluded.

Mr. Townshend's books are about equal in number to those
of the Literary Society, but are wider in the range of their
topics. His collection is of the kind to be expected in the
library of a gentleman of wealth, great culture, and variety
of tastes. Fiction—both English and Foreign,—General

Literature, and the Sciences, are found in tolerably impartial proportions. Many of the volumes are extremely well bound.

As some of the works, more particularly those of the Townshend section, are very valuable because of their rarity and intrinsic excellence, the Librarian, by the decision of the Committee, may at his discretion refuse to readers permission to remove them from the Museum.

The Literary Society's Catalogue has been out of print for many years; and that of the Townshend books, issued at the time of their acquisition by the Trustees of the Museum, was prepared upon a plan little suited to general use. Hence the want of a good general alphabetical list of the united collections has been felt by almost all readers.

The compilers of the present Catalogue are far from supposing that they have produced a faultless work; but the consciousness of the pains and efforts they have expended upon it lead them to hope it will prove a fairly reliable guide to the Museum Library, and that readers will find their long felt grievance substantially removed.

CATALOGUE.

ABBOT, The ....*Scott.*
Abbott, Major J.—Heraut to Khiva, &c., Journey from, 2 vols.
Abeillard and Heloisa, Lives of, 4to. ....*Berington.*
Abel Allnutt, 3 vols. ....*Morier.*
Abell, Mrs.—Napoleon at St. Helena, Recollections of
Abernethy, John, Memoirs of, 2 vols. ....*Macilwain.*
Abipones, Account of the, 3 vols. ....*Dobrizhoffen.*
Absenteeism ....*Morgan.*
Abyssinia, Captive Missionary in ....*Stern.*
———— Life in, 2 vols. ....*Parkins.*
———— Life and Adventures in, 2 vols. ....*Pearce.*
———— Nile Tributaries of ....*Baker.*
———— Story of the Captives of ....*Blanc.*
———— Three Years' Residence in ....*Gobat.*
Academy for Grown Horsemen, 4to., 1787 ....*Gambado.*
Achilli, Giacinto—Inquisition, Dealings with the
Acts and Monuments of the Church, 3 vols. fo., 1684 ...*Foxe.*
———————————————— 8 vols., 1839 ...... ,,
Acts of Parliament of Scotland, 1427 to 1707.
Acute Diseases, On, 1687 ....*Pechey.*
A. D.'s Hindostan, Tour through
Adams, John—Anecdotes and Bonmots.
———— Robert—Tombuctoo, Captivity and Residence at, 4to.
———— Thomas—Devil's Banket, (sermons) 1614.

B

Agricultural Chemistry, Lectures on, 4to. ....*Davy.*

———— Society of England, vols. 1—5, 7—14.

Agrippa, H. C.—Occult Philosophy, &c., Three Books of, 1651.

——————————————————— Fourth Book, 1783.

Aids to Reflection ....*S. T. Coleridge.*

Aikin, Arthur—Wales, North, Tour through

——- J.—Manchester, Description of Country round, 4to.

———— Letters to His Son, 2 vols.

——- Lucy—Addison, Joseph, Life of, 2 vols.

———— Elizabeth, Memoirs of Court of, 2 vols.

———— James I. ,, ,, 2 vols.

———— Charles I. ,, ,, 2 vols.

Ainsworth, Henry—Pentateuch, Annotations to, folio, 1639.

———- W. Harrison—Constable of the Tower.

———————- Guy Fawkes.

—————————- Jack Sheppard, 3 vols.

———————- Lancashire Witches, 3 vols.

———————- Old Saint Paul's.

——————- Tower of London.

———— R.—Dictionary, Latin

Aiton, J. —Messiah, Mahomet, and the Pope, Lands of, 2 vols.

Akenside, Mark—Pleasures of Imagination.

Akerman, J. Y.—Numismatic Chronicle, 1838 to 1845, 3 vols.

————————————————— July, 1847.

Albania to Constantinople, Journey through, 4to. ....*Hobhouse.*

Albemarle, Duke of, Marq. of Rockingham, Memoirs of, 2 vols.

Albert N'yanza, Discovery of the, 2 vols. ....*Baker.*

Albigenses, Crusades against the, History of ....*Sismondi.*

Alceste, Voyage of the ....*McLeod.*

Alcoholic Liquors, Use and Abuse of ....*Carpenter.*

Alet and La Grand Chartreuse, 2 vols. ....*Lancelot.*

Alexander the Great, History of, 2 vols. ....*Rufus.*

———— the First of Russia, Life of ....*Lloyd.*

———— Last Days of, and First of Nicholas ....*Leigh.*

Alexander, Sir J. E.—Canada as it was, is, and may be.

————— —————— Africa, Colonies of Western, 2 vols.

————— William—Women, History of, 2 vols., 4to.

Alfieri, Victor, Memoirs of, 2 vols.

Alford, Dean—The Queen's English.

Algiers, Residence in, 4to. ....*Pananti.*

Alhambra, The, 2 vols. ....*Irving.*

Ali, Mrs. Meer Hassan—Mussulmauns of India, 2 vols.

Alice, or the Mysteries, 3 vols. ....*Lytton.*

Alice's Adventures in Wonderland ....*Carroll.*

Alison, Archibald—Taste, Nature and Principles of, 4to.

————— Europe, History of, 1789 to 1815, 10 vols.

——— ——— ——— ——————— 1815 to 1852, 9 vols.

————— Marlborough, Military Life of Duke of

————— Population, Principles of, 2 vols.

All the Year Round, vols. 1 and 2, 4—18.

Allen, John—Judaism, Modern, Account of.

—— Joseph—British Navy, Battles of, 2 vols.

—— William, Memoirs of ....*Sherman.*

Alleyne, James—Dispensatory, English, 1733.

Almanac, Comic, 1838 to 1848, 1851 to 1853, 6 vols.

Alma Mater, 2 vols.

Alpenstock, or Sketches of Swiss Scenery ....*Latrobe.*

Alps, Scrambles amongst, in 1860—1869 ....*Whymper.*

—— of Savoy, &c., Travels through

Altars, Hearths, and Homes ....*Moultrie.*

Alton Locke, 2 vols. ....*C. Kingsley.*

Alvensleben, Baron von—With Maximilian in Mexico.

Amazon, Burning of the, a Poem ....*Townshend.*

————— and River Negro, Travels on the ....*Wallace.*

Ambarvalia, Poems ....*Burbidge and Clough.*

Amber Witch, The, translated from the German.

Ambler, J. P.—Spiritual Teacher, Lectures by Spirits.

America, Ancient Institutions of, 2 vols. ....*Humboldt.*

America, New Discovery of a large Country in, 1699..*Hennepin.*
———— European Settlements in, Account of, 2 vols...*Burke.*
———— History of, 4 vols. ....*Robertson.*
———— Travels in ....*Chastellux.*
———— ———— 3 vols. ....*Lambert.*
———— ———— ....*Lewis and Clarke.*
———— Diary in, 3 vols. ....*Marryat.*
———— Journal of a Residence in ....*Butler.*
———— Memorable Days in ....*Faux.*
———— Men and Manners in, 2 vols.
––———— British, 2 vols. ....*McGregor.*
———— North, Travels in, 3 vols. ....*Hall.*
———— ———— 2 vols. ....*Lyell.*
———— ———— 2 vols. ....*Murray.*
———— ———— 4 vols. ....*Rochefoucault.*
———— ———— ....*Carver.*
———— ———— Three Years in, 2 vols. ....*Stuart.*
———— ———— Forest Scenes in ....*Head.*
———— ———— Wanderings of Artist among Indians of..*Kane.*
———— ———— Coast of, Discoveries on
———— ———— United States of, Sketches of the...*Beaujour.*
———— ———— ———— Excursion to,1794.*Wansey.*
———— New, 2 vols. ....*Dixon.*
———— Central, Incidents of Travels in, 2 vols. ...*Stephens.*
———— West of, Travels in ....*Michaux.*
———— South, Travels in, 2 vols. ....*Depon.*
———— ———— Wanderings in, 4to. ....*Waterton.*
American in Paris during the Summer ....*J. Janin.*
Americans, Domestic Manners of, 2 vols. ....*Trollope.*
American States, Observations on the Commerce of...*Sheffield.*
———— South, Journal of the Station, 1820-2, 2 vols...*Hall.*
———— Notes, 2 vols. ....*Dickens.*
Amoor, Upper and Lower, Travels in the Regions of...*Atkinson.*
Anacharsis in Greece, Travels of, 7 vols.

Andromeda, and other Poems ....*C. Kingsley.*
Anecdotes of the Aristocracy, 2 vols. ....*Burke.*
——————— Books and Men ....*Spence.*
——————— some Distinguished Persons, 5 vols. ...*Seward.*
——————— Earl of Chatham, 4 vols.
——————— Heroic Women ....*Du Broca.*
——————— Biographical, of William Hogarth ....*Nicholls.*
——————— Literary, of the Eighteenth Century ....*Nichols.*
——————— of Literature and Scarce Books, 6 vols. ......*Beloe.*
——————— Miscellaneous, *temp.* Charles II. to Anne ...*Malcolm.*
——————— of Monkeys.
——————— of the Russian Empire.
——————— of the Upper Ten Thousand, 2 vols. ......*Berkeley.*
——————— and Biographical Sketches, vol. i. ....*Hawkins.*
——————— and Bonmots ....*Adams.*
Angelo, Michael, Life of ....*Duppa.*
Angels, Treatise on, 1613 ....*Salkeld.*
Angerstein Collection in National Gallery, Catalogue of
Anglo-Saxons, History of ....*Turner.*
Angler, The Complete ....*Walton and Cotton.*
Animal Biography, 3 vols. ....*Bingley.*
—————— World, Strange Stories of the ....*Timbs.*
—————— Economy of the, 2 vols. ....*Swedenborg.*
—————— Kingdom, 15 vols. and Index ....*Cuvier.*
Animals in Menageries ....*Swainson.*
—————— Geography of .... ,,
—————— Habits of .... ,,
—————— Habits and Instincts of, 2 vols. ....*Kirby.*
—————— British Vertebrate, Manual of ....*Jenyns.*
Animated Nature, History of, 8 vols. ....*Goldsmith.*
Annals for Banks of Savings.
Annals of the Parish.
Anne of Geierstein ....*Scott.*
—— Grey, 3 vols.

Atlas of the World ....*Wyld.*
——— —— ——— ....*Wilkinson.*
—— of England and Wales, folio ....*Cary.*
Attaché, The, or Sam Slick in England, 2 vols. ...*Halliburton.*
Aubrey, John—Fatality, Apparitions, &c., Miscellanies upon
Audubon, the Naturalist in the New World ....*St. John.*
Augustine, St., Confessions of, 1679.
Aunt Margaret's Troubles.
Aurora Leigh, a Poem ....*E. B. Browning.*
——— Floyd ....*Braddon.*
Austen, Jane, Memoirs of
——————— Emma, 3 vols.
——————— Mansfield Park, 3 vols.
——————— Northanger Abbey and Persuasion, 4 vols.
——————— Pride and Prejudice, 3 vols.
——————— Sense and Sensibility, 3 vols.
Austin, Mrs.—Orleans, Duchess of, Memoirs of
——————— Smith, Rev. Sidney, Memoirs & Letters of, 2 vols.
——— Sarah—Story without an end.
——— Arthur—*See*, Wilson, John.
——— W. S. and J. Ralph—Lives of the Poets-Laureate.
Australia as it is ....*Lancelot.*
——— Discoveries in, 2 vols. ....*Stokes.*
———————————— 2 vols. ....*Grey.*
——— Eastern, Three Expeditions to, 2 vols. ...*Mitchell.*
——— Overland Expedition into ....*Leichhardt.*
——— Picture of
——— Three Colonies of ....*Sidney.*
——— Central, Discoveries in, 2 vols. ....*Eyre.*
————————— Expedition into, 2 vols. ....*Sturt.*
——— North West and Western, Travels in, 2 vols. ...*Grey.*
——— South, and its Mines............................*Dutton.*
————————— Description of
Australian Exploring Expeditions in 1860 ....*Burke.*

Bacon, F. (Lord Verulam)—Essays, with Annotations. *Whateley.*
———————————— Life and Miscellaneous Works of
———————————— Novum Organum, &c.
———————————— Works of, 17 vols.
———————————————— 10 vols.
———————————————— 9 vols.
Baffin's Bay, Journal of Voyage in, 2 vols. ....*Sutherland.*
————— Whaling Cruise to ....*Markham.*
Bailey, N.—Dictionary, English Etymological, folio, 1736.
————— P. J.—Festus, a Poem.
————————— The Mystic and other Poems.
Baillie, Joanna—Dramas, 3 vols.
————————— Dramatic and Poetical Works.
————— ——— Miscellaneous Plays.
————————— Plays of, 4 vols., 1798.
————————— Series of Plays, 2 vols.
Baines, Edward, Junr.—Cotton Manufacture, History of
————— Thomas—Africa, Explorations in South West
Baird, Sir David, Life of
Baker, H. B.—French Society, Fronde to Revolution, 2 vols.
————— Sir S. W.—Ismailia, 2 vols.
————————— Abyssinia, Nile Tributaries of
————————— Albert N'yanza, Discovery of the, 2 vols.
Bakewell, Robert—Geology, Introduction to
Balcan, Journey across, 2 vols. ....*Keppel.*
Balder, a Poem, part i.
Baldwin, Wm. C.—African Hunting.
Ballads and Tales.
Ballou, A.—Spirit Manifestations.
Baltic, Letters from the Shores of
————— Northern Summer Tour round, 4to. ....*Carr.*
————— Residence on the Shores of, 2 vols.
————— Tour round ....*Wraxall.*
Banim, John, Life of ....*Murray.*

Banks, G. L.—Blondin's Life and Performances.

Bar, The, a Poem.

Barbary, Western, The Wild Tribes of ....*Hay.*

Barbauld, Mrs. A. L.—Richardson, S., Correspondence of
——————————— Works of, 2 vols.

Barca, Madame de la—Mexico, Life in

Barchester Towers, 3 vols. ....*Trollope.*

Barclay, John—On Life and Organization.

Bareith, Margravine of, Memoirs of, 2 vols.

Baretti, Guiseppe—Dictionary, Italian

Barham, R. H. D.—Ingoldsby Legends, 3 vols.
——————————— Hook, T. E., Life and Remains of, 2 vols.

Baring, G. S.—Old Testament Characters, Legends of, 2 vols.
——————— Were-Wolves, Book of

Barlow, J.—Physiology and Philosophy, Connection between

Barnaby Rudge ....*Dickens.*

Barnum, Thomas, Life of

Barrera, Madame de—Gems and Jewels, History of
——————————— Rachel, Memoirs of, 2 vols.

Barrett, E. S.—The Heroine, 3 vols.

Barrington, Sir J.—Personal Sketches of his own Times, 3 vols.

Barrow, Isaac—Theological Works of, 8 vols.
—————— Sir John—Africa, Travels in Southern, 2 vols., 4to.
——————————— China, Travels in, 4to.
——————————— Arctic Regions, Voyages into
——————————— Autobiographical Memoir of
——————————— Anson, Life of Admiral George
——————————— Bounty, History of the Mutiny of the
——————————— Drake, Life and Voyages of Sir Francis

Barruel, Abbé—Jacobinism, History of, 4 vols.

Barry, Herbert—Ivan at Home, or Pictures of Russian Life.
————James—Painting, Lectures on
——————————— Pictures painted by, Description of (pamphlet.)

Barth, Dr. H.—Africa, Travels in Central, 5 vols.

Bartlett, W. H.—Forty Days in the Desert.
———————— Nile Boat.
Barton, Bernard—Household Verses.
——————— Poems of, 2 vols.
——————— Juvenile Scrap Book, 1838.
Bases of Belief ....*Miall.*
Bashan, The Giant Cities of ....*Porter.*
Basil ....*Collins.*
Basile, G.—The Pentamarone, translated by Taylor.
Bastile, History of the
Bate, Dr.—Dispensatory, 1720.
Bates, H. W.—Naturalist on the Amazon.
Bath, Excursions from ....*Warner.*
—— Guide, The New, 1774.
—— Society, Memoirs of the, 5 vols.
—— Waters, Memoirs on the, 1697.
Bathing Cold, History of, 1722 ....*Floyer and Barnard.*
Bathurst, Bishop, Memoirs of, 2 vols.
—————————————— & Correspondence of...*Thistlewaite.*
Battle of Life ....*Dickens.*
—— of Paraquay ....*Southey.*
Battles of the World, Fifteen Decisive, 2 vols. ....*Creasy.*
Baviad and Meviad ....*Gifford.*
Bean Flower and Pea Blossom ....*Nodier.*
Beatson, Alex.—St. Helena, Tracts relative to Island of, 4to.
——————— Tippoo Sultaun, View of the War with, 4to.
——————— R.—Naval & Military Memoirs of Gt. Britain, 6 vols.
Beattie, James—Critical Essays, 4to.
——————— Dissertations, Moral and Critical, 4to.
——————— Minstrel and other Poems.
——————— Life of, 2 vols., 4to. ....*Forbes.*
——————— with Somerville & Johnson—The Minstrel, &c.
——————— Campbell Thomas, Life and Letters of, 3 vols.
Beauchesne, A. de—Louis the Seventeenth, Life of, 2 vols.

c

Bell, Currer—*See* ,, Charlotte.
—— Ellis— ,, ,, Emily.
—— Major J.—Universal History, Compendious View of, folio.
—— Sir Charles—On the Hand, as evincing Design.
——————— Letters of
—— R.—Poets, Eminent English, 2 vols.
—— Robert —Ladder of Gold.
—— John—Italy, Observations on, 2 vols.
Bellamy, George Anne, Apology for the Life of, 6 vols.
Bellendenius, Translation by Beloe of the Preface to ...*Parr.*
Belles Lettres, Method of Studying, 4 vols. ....*Rollin.*
Bellini, Laurentius—Fevers, Mechanical Account of, 1720
Beloe, W.—Anecdotes of Literature and Scarce Books, 6 vols.
——————— Sexagenarian, or Recollections of a Literary Life.
Belsham, Thomas—Mind, Philosophy of the
——————— William—Great Britain, History of, 2 vols.
Belshazzar, a Dramatic Poem ....*Milman.*
Belzoni, G.—Egypt and Nubia, Researches in, 4to., plates folio.
Bench and Bar, 2 vols.
Benevolus, Hilaris—Pleasures of Human Life, 1807.
Benger, Miss—Anne Boleyn, Memoirs of, 2 vols.
——— ——— Queen of Bohemia, Memoirs of, 2 vols.
Bennet, J. Henry—Mentone, &c., as Winter Climates.
Bennett, Fredk. D.—Whaling Voyage Round the Globe, 2 vols.
——— George —New South Wales, Wanderings in, 2 vols.
——— Solomon—The Constancy of Israel.
——— W. C.—Queen Eleanor's Vengeance and other Poems.
——————— Poems.
Benson, Robert—Corsica, Sketches of
Bentham, Jas.—Ely, Hist. of Collegiate Church of, 2 vols., 4to.
——— Jeremy—Defence of Usury.
——————— Works of, 11 vols.
Bentinck, Lord George, Political Biography of ...*B. D'Israeli.*
Bentley, Dr. Richard, Life of, 4to. ....*Monk.*

Beppo, a Poem, 1818 ....*Byron.*

Berington, Joseph—Abeillard and Heloisa, Lives of, 4to.

———————— Literary History of the Middle Ages, 4to.

Berkeley, Bishop—On Human Knowledge, 1734.

———— - Grantley—Anecdotes of Upper Ten Thousand, 2 vols.

——————— Life and Recollections of, 4 vols.

Berkenhout, Dr.—Letters to his Son.

Bernard, Sir Thomas—Comforts of Old Age.

Bernier, Francis—Mogul Empire, Travels in the, 2 vols.

Berquin, Madame—Children's Friend, 6 vols.

Berry, Miss, Journal of, 1783—1852, 3 vols.

Berwick on Tweed, History of ....*Fuller.*

———— Marshal Duke of, Memoirs of, 1716—1734, 2 vols.

———— Rev. E.—Apollonius of Tyana.

Bethell, Hon. Augusta—Helen in Switzerland.

Betrothed, The ....*Scott.*

———————— Lovers, 2 vols. ....*Manzoni.*

Better Self ....*Friswell.*

Bewick Collector, The ....*Hugo.*

———— Thomas —British Birds, History of, 2 vols.

——————— Quadrupeds,   ,,

Bible, History of, 2 vols., folio, 1733 ....*Stackhouse.*

—— in Spain, 3 vols. ....*Borrow.*

Bibliolatry, an Essay.......................................*Hughes.*

Bibliotheca Londinensis, 1814—1846.

Bidlake, John—The Year, a Poem.

Bidulph, Miss Sidney, Memoirs of

Bigland, J.—History, Ancient & Modern, Letters on Study of

Bingham, J. Elliot—China, Expedition to, 2 vols.

Bingley, Rev. W.—Animal Biography, 3 vols.

Biographia Britannica, vols. i.—v., folio.

———— Dramatica, 2 vols. ....*Jones.*

———— Literaria, 2 vols. ....*S. T. Coleridge.*

Biographical Dictionary, 1799.

Blair, Hugh—Rhetoric and Belles Lettres, Lectures on, 2 vols.
———— Sermons, 3 vols.
—— Mrs. Ferguson—The Henwife.
Blake, Rev. J. W. J.—Long Vacation in Picture Galleries.
Blakelock, R.—Euclid, Elements of
Blakesley, Rev. R. W.—Aristotle, Life of
Blanc, L.—History of the Ten Years from 1830 to 1840, 2 vols.
—— Dr.—Story of the Captives (Abyssinia).
Blanchard, Laman—Sketches from Life, 3 vols.
Blaney, Lord—Spain and France, Forced Journey thro', 2 vols.
Blank Book of a Small Colleger.
Bleak House, 2 vols. ....*Dickens*.
Blessington, Countess of—Idler in France, 2 vols.
——————————————— Italy, 3 vols.
——————————————— Life and Correspondence ..*Madden*.
Bligh, Capt. W.—Mutiny of the Bounty, Narrative of the, 4to.
Blome, Richd.—Geographical Description of the World, 1670.
Blomefield, Fras.—Norfolk, Topographical History of, 11 vols.
Blondin, Life and Performances of ....*Banks*.
Bloom, Rev. J. H.—Castleacre, History of Castle and Priory at
Bloxam, Matthew H.—Architecture, Gothic Ecclesiastical
Blucher, Marshal, Life and Campaigns of ....*Marston*.
Blue Book, Royal, 1862 and 1865, 2 vols.
Blumenthal, Madame de—De Zieten, General, Life of, 2 vols.
Blunt, John J.—Italy, Vestiges of Ancient Manners in
—— Rev. H.—Jacob, Lectures on
——————— St. Peter, ,,
Blythedale Romance, 2 vols. ....*Hawthorne*.
Boaden, James—Jordan, Mrs., Life of, 2 vols.
——————— Kemble, J. P. ,, 2 vols.
——————— Siddons, Mrs., ,, 2 vols.
Bocages and the Vines, Summer among, 2 vols. ......*Costello*.
Bode, J. E.—Ballads from Herodotus.
Bodleian Library, Selection of Letters from, 3 vols.

Boerhaave, H., Aphorisms of, 8 vols., 1754 ....*Swieten.*
———— ———— Chemistry, Elements of, 4to., 1735.
———————— Physic, Method of Studying, 1719.
Bohemia, Queen of, Memoirs of, 2 vols. ....*Benger.*
Boisgelins, Louis de—Malta, Ancient and Modern, 2 vols., 4to.
Bokhara, Mission to, 2 vols. ....*Wolff.*
———— Travels into, 3 vols. ....*Burnes.*
———— and Hindostan, Travels in, 2 vols. ......*Moorcroft.*
Boleyn, Anne, Memoirs of, 2 vols. ....*Benger.*
Bolingbroke, Lord—Letters on the Study and use of History.
———————— Letter to Sir W. Windham.
———— ———— Works of, 8 vols.
Bombay, Overland Journey to ....*Roberts.*
Bonaparte, Napoleon, Life of
———— ———————— 9 vols. ....*Scott.*
———— ———— ——— Memoirs of, 4 vols. ....*Bourrienne.*
———————————— ....*D'Abrantes.*
———— ———— Historical Memoirs of, 1815 ...*O'Meara.*
———————— Private Life, Memoirs of ..*De Chaboulon.*
———— ——— at Dresden, Intercepted Letters to
———— ———— Narrative of the Surrender of..*Maitland.*
·————————— Private Life of, Journal of ...*Las Cases.*
———————— at St. Helena, Recollections of.*Mrs. Abell.*
———— ————————— 4 vols. ....*Montholon.*
———— ————— ———— Treatment of
———— ————— in Exile, 2 vols. ....*O'Meara.*
———————— Captivity of ....*Forsyth.*
———— ——— Secret History of Cabinet of..*Goldsmith.*
———— —— ——— and the French People.
———— ———— France during the Reign of, 7 vols.
·———— ———— Letters from Paris during Last Reign of
———— Lucien—Charlemagne, a Poem, 2 vols., 4to.
———— Louis—Holland, On the Government of, 3 vols.
Bonchamp, Marchioness of, Memoirs of

Bonney, Rev. H. K.—Fotheringay, Historic Notices of
Bonnycastle, Richard H.—Canadas in 1841, 2 vols.
———————————— Newfoundland in 1842, 2 vols.
Book of Snobs ....*Thackeray.*
Booth, David—English Composition, Principles of
Borderers, The ....*Cooper.*
Borneo, Adventures in
——— Expedition to, 2 vols. ....*Keppel.*
——— and the Indian Archipelago ....*Marryatt.*
Boroughs of Great Britain, History of the, 3 vols.
Borrow, George—Bible in Spain, 3 vols.
——————— Lavengro; the Scholar, Gipsy, Priest, 3 vols.
——————— Romany Rye, 2 vols.
——————— Wild Wales, 3 vols.
——————— Zincali, or the Gypsies of Spain.
Boston, History of ....*Thompson.*
Boswell, Jas.—Johnson, Dr. Sam., Life of (Croker's ed.) 5 vols.
——————— Letters of
Bosworth Field, Battle of ....*Hutton.*
Botanic Garden, 4to., 1791 ....*E. Darwin.*
Botanical Dictionary, Pocket ....*Paxton.*
Botanicum Officinale (Herbal), 1722 ....*Miller.*
Botany, Introduction to ....*Lee.*
——— Descriptive and Physiological ....*Henslow.*
Boteler, Thomas—Africa, Voyage to, 2 vols.
Bothwell, a Poem ....*Aytoun.*
Botta, Carlo—Italy, History of, during reign of Napoleon, 2 vols.
Boulton and Watt, Lives of ....*Smiles.*
Bounty, Mutiny on Board of H.M.S. ....*Barrow.*
———————— ——————— 4to. ....*Bligh.*
——— Mutineers of ....*Lady Belcher.*
Bourne, H. R. Fox—English Merchants, 2 vols.
——— Vincent—Poems, 2 vols.
Bourrienne, F. de—Napoleon Bonaparte, Memoirs of, 4 vols.

Boutell, Rev. Charles—Monumental Brasses and Slabs.
Bowles, William L.—Poetical Works of
Boyd, Belle (Mrs. Hardinge)—In Camp and Prison.
Boyle, Robert—Works of, 5 vols., folio, 1744.
Boy's Voyage Round the World ....*Smiles.*
Braam, A. E. van—China, Dutch Embassy to, 2 vols.
Bracebridge Hall, 2 vols. ....*Irving.*
Bracelets, The ....*Edgeworth.*
Braddon, Miss—Aurora Floyd.
———————— Captain of the Vulture.
Brady, J.—Clavis Calendaria; Analysis of the Calendar, 2 vols.
Brand, John—Antiquities, Popular, 2 vols., 4to.
Brassey, Thomas—Life and Labours of, 1805—1870 ...*Helps.*
Brayley, E. W.—Londiniana (Reminiscences of London) 4 vols.
Brayley & Britton—Westminster, History of Ancient Palace of
Breay, Rev. J. G., Memoirs of
Breeze from the Great Salt Lake ....*Ollivant.*
Bremer, Frederika—Diary of
———————————— H— Family.
———————————— Hertha.
———————————— Homes of the New World, 3 vols.
———————————— Nina, 2 vols.
———————————— President's Daughter.
———————————— Strife and Peace.
Brewster, Sir D.—Sir Isaac Newton, Life of
———————————— More Worlds than One.
———————————— Natural Magic, Letters on
———————————— Optics.
———————————— Stereoscope, The
Bridal of Triermain and other Poems ....*Scott.*
Bride of Abydos ....*Byron.*
Bride of Lammermoor ....*Scott.*
Bridges, Rev. Charles—Graham, Miss M. J., Memoir of

Bridgwater Treatises, 13 vols., viz. :—
    Bell on the Hand as evincing Design.
    Buckland on Geology and Mineralogy, 2 vols.
    Chalmers on the Constitution of Man, 2 vols.
    Kidd on the Physical Condition of Man.
    Kirby on the Habits and Instincts of Animals, 2 vols.
    Prout on Chemistry, Meteorology, &c.
    Roget on Animal and Vegetable Physiology, 2 vols.
    Whewell on Astronomy and General Physics.
    Babbage—Ninth Treatise, a Fragment.
Brigadier Frederic ....*Erckman.*
Brigand Life in Italy, 2 vols. ....*Maffei.*
Brightwell, Cecilia L.—Opie, Amelia, Life of
Britain, Eminent Men of, 3 vols.
Britannia, 3 vols., folio, translated by Gough ....*Camden.*
British Association, Lithograph Signatures of, 4to., 1833.
British Colonies, Letters on ....*St. John.*
British Critic, 1793—1835, 82 vols.
———————— 1836—1843, in parts.
——— Empire, Wealth and Power of, 4to. ....*Colquhoun.*
——— Guiana, History of, 2 vols. ....*Dalton.*
——— Museum, Synopsis of Contents of, 1818, pamphlet.
——— Navy, Abstracts of, 4to.
——————— Battles of, 2 vols. ....*Allen.*
——— Poets, Aldine and Chiswick editions, 50 vols.
——————— Bell's edition, in two cases, 108 vols.
——————— Bohn's edition, 4 vols.
——————— Specimens of
——— Statesmen, 7 vols.
Britton, John—Fonthill Abbey, Illustrations of, 4to.
————— Peterborough Cathedral, History of, 4to.
Broad Grins ....*Colman.*
Broad Stone of Honour ; Rules for Gentlemen.
Broderip, W. J.—Zoological Recreations.

Brodie, Sir Benjamin—Physiological Enquiries, 2 vols.

———————————————————— Researches.

——— Peter B.—Fossil Insects, History of

Brooke, Arthur de C.—Lapland and Sweden, Winter in, 4to.

——— Sir James—Sarawak, Ten Years in

——— T. H.—St. Helena, History of

Brookes, R.—Physic, Practice of, 2 vols., 1763.

——— Richard—General Gazetteer, abridged, 1796.

Brooks, Shirley—Russians of the South.

——————————— Sooner or Later, 2 vols.

Brontë, Anne—Agnes Grey.

——— Charlotte, Life of, 2 vols. .... *Gaskell.*

——————————— Jane Eyre.

——————————— The Professor, 2 vols.

——————————— Shirley.

——— Emily—Wuthering Heights.

Brougham, Lord, Life and Times of, 3 vols.

——————— Men of Letters of George III., 2 vols.

——————— Statesmen of George III.

——————— Political Philosophy, 3 vols.

——————— and Lyndhurst, Lives of ....*Campbell.*

Broughton, S. D.—Portugal, Spain, &c., Letters from

Brown, Dr. J.—Estimate of Manners of the Times, 2 vols., 1758.

——— John—North West Passage and Search for Franklin.

——— John W.—Leonardo da Vinci, Life of

——— Sir T.—Works of, 4 vols.

——————— Religio Medici and Digby's Observations, 1682.

——— Dr. Thomas—Mind, Philosophy of the

——— T. the younger—Intercepted Letters; Political Poems.

——— Capt. Thomas—Conchologist's Text Book.

——— C. B.—Edgar Huntley, or the Sleep Walker.

——————— Wieland, 3 vols.

——— William—Antiquities of the Jews, 2 vols.

Browne, Moses—Works, and Rest of the Creation.

Browning, Elizabeth B.—Aurora Leigh, a Poem.
——————————— Poems, 2 vols.
—————————————— before Congress.
———————— Robert—Christmas Eve and Easter Day.
——————————— Dramatis Personæ, Poems.
———————————— Men and Women, 2 vols.
———————— W. S.—Huguenots, History of the
Brownson, O. A.—Charles Elwood, or the Infidel Converted.
Bruce, James, Life of, 4to. ....*Murray.*
——————— Nile, Travels to Discover Source of, 7 vols.
——————————————————— Abridgement of ...*Shaw.*
———————— Peter H., Memoirs of, 4to.
Brunton, Mary—Emmeline, with other Pieces.
Bryan, Michael—Painters and Engravers, Dictionary of
Brydges, Sir E.—Ruminator; a series of Essays, 2 vols.
Brydone, P.—Sicily and Malta, Tour through, 2 vols.
Bubbles from the Brunnens of Nassau ....*Head.*
Buccaneers of America, History of
Buchan, William—Domestic Medicine.
Buchanan, Rev. C.—Christian Researches in Asia.
——————————— Colonial Ecclesiastical Establishment.
——————————— Memoirs of, 2 vols.
Buckingham, Duke of—Court & Cabinets of George III., 4 vols.
————— ——————— Court of England, 1811—1820, 2 vols.
———————— James Silk—Autobiography of, 2 vols.
——————————————— Mesopotamia, Travels in, 4to.
Buckland, Rev. William—Reliquiæ Diluvianæ, 4to.
——————————————— Geology and Mineralogy, 2 vols.
———————— F.—Natural History, Curiosities of, 4 vols.
Buckle, Henry—Civilization, History of, 2 vols.
Buckler, J. C. & C. A.—Architecture of St. Alban's & Eltham.
Buenos Ayres, History of ....*Parish.*
——————————————— ....*Wilcocke.*
——————————— Journey from, 2 vols. ....*Andrews.*

29

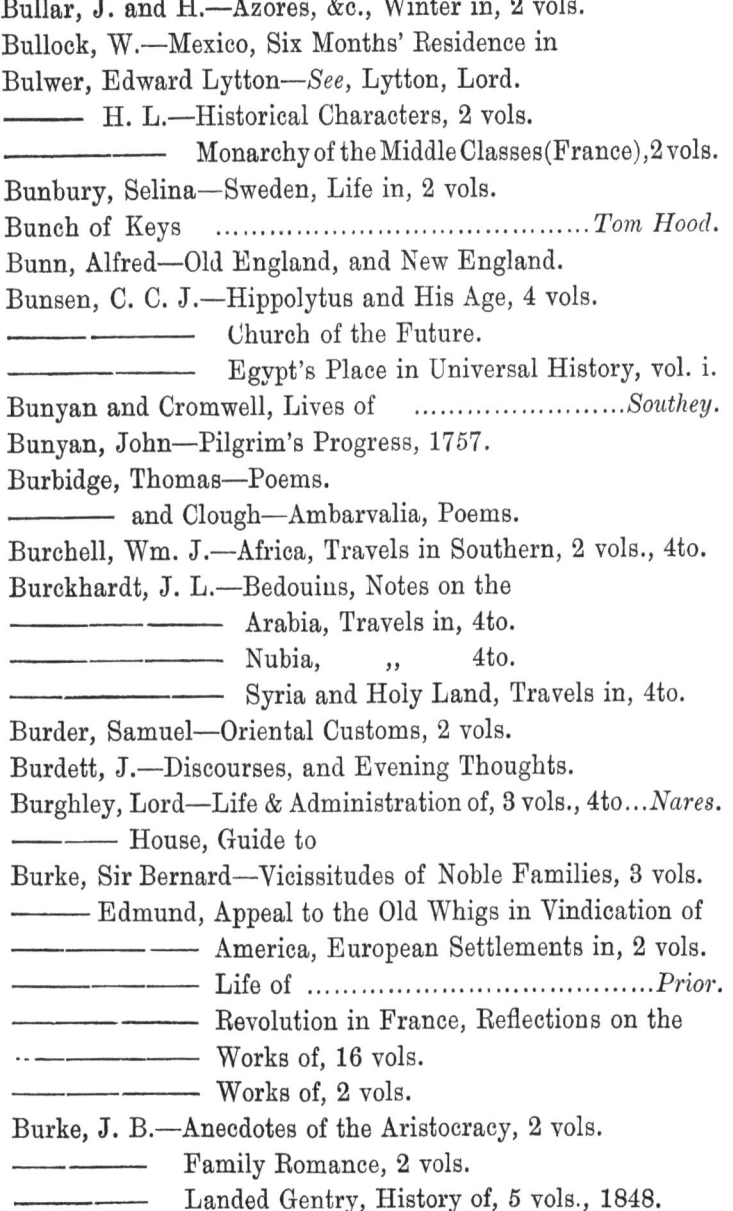

Bullar, J. and H.—Azores, &c., Winter in, 2 vols.
Bullock, W.—Mexico, Six Months' Residence in
Bulwer, Edward Lytton—*See*, Lytton, Lord.
———— H. L.—Historical Characters, 2 vols.
——————— Monarchy of the Middle Classes(France),2 vols.
Bunbury, Selina—Sweden, Life in, 2 vols.
Bunch of Keys ....*Tom Hood.*
Bunn, Alfred—Old England, and New England.
Bunsen, C. C. J.—Hippolytus and His Age, 4 vols.
———— ———— Church of the Future.
———— ———— Egypt's Place in Universal History, vol. i.
Bunyan and Cromwell, Lives of ....*Southey.*
Bunyan, John—Pilgrim's Progress, 1757.
Burbidge, Thomas—Poems.
———— and Clough—Ambarvalia, Poems.
Burchell, Wm. J.—Africa, Travels in Southern, 2 vols., 4to.
Burckhardt, J. L.—Bedouins, Notes on the
———— ———— Arabia, Travels in, 4to.
———— ———— Nubia, ,, 4to.
———— ———— Syria and Holy Land, Travels in, 4to.
Burder, Samuel—Oriental Customs, 2 vols.
Burdett, J.—Discourses, and Evening Thoughts.
Burghley, Lord—Life & Administration of, 3 vols., 4to...*Nares.*
———— House, Guide to
Burke, Sir Bernard—Vicissitudes of Noble Families, 3 vols.
———— Edmund, Appeal to the Old Whigs in Vindication of
———— ———— America, European Settlements in, 2 vols.
———— ———— Life of ....*Prior.*
———— ———— Revolution in France, Reflections on the
·· ———— ———— Works of, 16 vols.
———— ———— Works of, 2 vols.
Burke, J. B.—Anecdotes of the Aristocracy, 2 vols.
———— Family Romance, 2 vols.
———— Landed Gentry, History of, 5 vols., 1848.

Burke, J. B.—Landed Gentry, Dictionary of, 1852.

———— ——— Romantic Records of the Aristocracy, 2 vols.

——— Peter—Romance of the Forum, 2 vols.

——— R. O'Hara—Australian Exploring Expeditions in 1860.

Burkitt, W.—Expository Notes on the Acts & Epistles, fo., 1703.

Burlesques .... *Thackeray.*

Burmah, Two Years' Imprisonment in ....*Gouger.*

Burmese War, Narrative of ....*Snodgrass.*

Burmhan Empire, Journal of a Residence in ....*Cox.*

Burnes, Sir Alex.—Bokhara, Travels into, 3 vols.

——— James—Sinde, Visit to the Court of

Burnet, Bishop—History of His Own Times, 6 vols.

———— ——— Reformation, History of the, 6 vols. & Index.

———— ——— Lives, Characters, & an Address to Posterity.

Burnett, George—Poland, View of

Burney, Dr. C.—Music, General History of, 4 vols., 4to.

———— ——— Memoirs of, 3 vols. ....*D'Arblay.*

——— Frances—Camilla, 5 vols.

———— ——— Cecilia, or Memoirs of an Heiress, 3 vols.

———— ——— Evelina, 2 vols.

———— ——— Wanderer, or Female Difficulties, 5 vols.

———— ——— *See,* D'Arblay, Madame

Burns, Robert—Works of, 4 vols.

———— ——— Poems, 2 vols.

———— ——— Reliques of ....*Cromek.*

———— ——— Essay on ....*Carlyle.*

Burnt Njal, Story of, 2 vols. ....*Dasent.*

Burritt, Elihu—Sparks from the Anvil.

Burton, Rev. E.—Rome, Description of Antiquities of, 2 vols.

——— Richd. F —Falconry in the Valley of the Indus.

———— ——— El Medinah & Mecca, Pilgrimage to, 3 vols.

——— Rev. J.—The Parish Priest, a Poem.

——— Robert—Anatomy of Melancholy, folio, 1624.

Bury, Baroness B. de—Germania; Courts, Camps, &c., 2 vols.

Bury, Charlotte—Family Records.
———————— Flirtation, 3 vols.
———————— Marriage in High Life, and Confessions.
———————— Trevelyan.
Bush, Richard J.—Reindeer Dogs, and Snow Shoes.
Butler, Bp.—Analogy of Religion, Natural and Revealed, 1736.
————— Works of, 2 vols.
————— Frances A.—America, Journal of a Residence in, 2 vols.
——————— Poems.
————— Charles—Reminiscences.
—————— Revolutions of the Empire of Germany.
————— Samuel—Hudibras, 1775.
————— Poetical Remains.
————— W. F.—Great Lone Land.
————— Wild North Land.
Buxton, Thomas F.—Memoirs of
—————————— The African Slave Trade.
—————————— Prison Discipline.
Byron, Lord—Correspondence of
————— Journal of Conversations at Pisa ......*Medwin.*
————— Last Days of ....*Parry.*
————— Last Journey to Greece ....*Gamba.*
————— Life and Letters of, 2 vols., 4to. ....*Moore.*
————— and His Contemporaries, 2 vols. ....*Hunt.*
————— Voyage of, to Corsica and Sardinia, pamphlet.
————— Poems, Original and Translated, 1808.
—————————— containing, Bride of Abydos, Giaour,
    Lament of Tasso, Manfred, Mazeppa, Ode
    to Bonaparte, Parisina, Prisoner of Chillon,
    Siege of Corinth, Werner.
————— Poetical Works of
————— Beppo.
————— Childe Harold, 2 vols.
————— Corsair.

Byron, Lord—Don Juan.
——————— English Bards, and Scotch Reviewers.
——————— Lara, and Jacqueline.
——————— Marino Faliero, and Prophecy of Dante.
——————— Sardanapalus; Cain; The Two Foscari.

CAILLIÉ, R.—Africa, Travels through Central, 2 vols.
Cain; a Dramatic Poem ....*Byron.*
Calabria Ulteriore, Six Months Residence in ....*Elmhirst.*
Calcutta to Europe, Journey from ....*Lushington.*
———— to the Mergui Archipelago, 4to. ....*Forrest.*
Caleb Williams, 3 vols. ....*Godwin.*
Caledonia, vol. i., 4to. ....*Chalmers.*
Calendar of Nature, 1839.
————- to Pleadings, Duc. Lanc., Hen. VIII. to Eliz., 3 vols. fo.
California, History of ....*Forbes.*
Calvary; a Poem, 2 vols. ....*Cumberland.*
Calvert, General—Journal and Correspondence of
Camarupa and Camalata, Loves of ....*Franklin.*
Cambrian Directory, 1800.
Cambridge, Conversations at
——————— County of, History of ....*Carter.*
——————— Prize Poems, 1813—1817.
——————— University, Book Rarities in ....*Hartshorne.*
——————————————— History of, 2 vols. ....*Dyer.*
——————————————— Privileges of, 2 vols. .... ,,
——————————————— On the Studies of ....*Sedgwick.*
——————————————— Calendar, 1859.
Cambridgeshire, Topographical Account of, 4to. ......*Lysons.*
Camden, Wm.—Britannia, 3 vols. folio, translated by Gough.
Camilla, 5 vols. ....*Burney.*
Camoens, Luis de—Lusiad, translated by Mickle.
——————————— Poems, translated by Strangford.
Camp and Prison, In ....*Mrs. Hardinge.*

33

Campaign of 1815 ....*Gourgaud.*
Campaigns of the British Army at Washington.
Campan, Madame—Marie Antoinette, Memoirs of, 2 vols.
Campbell, Duncan—Life and Adventures of, 1720.
———— Dr. George—On the Miracles.
————— John—Lost among the Afghans.
———— Dr. J.—Admirals, Lives of, 4 vols.
———————————————— 8 vols., continued by Yorke.
—————— Gt. Britain, Political Survey of, 2 vols., 4to.
———— Rev. John—Africa, Travels in South, 2 vols.
———— Major General John—Khondistan, Wild Tribes of
———— Lord—Brougham and Lyndhurst, Lives of
—————— Chief Justices, Lives of, 3 vols.
——————— Lord Chancellors, Lives of, 7 vols.
———— Thomas—Gertrude of Wyoming & other Poems, 4to.
—————— Life and Letters of, 3 vols. ......*Beattie.*
—————— Letters from the South, 2 vols.
—————— Pilgrim of Glencoe.
—————— Pleasures of Hope.
—————— Theodric and other Poems.
Can You Forgive Her? 2 vols. ....*Trollope.*
Canada as it was, is, and may be ....*Alexander.*
——— Conquest of, 2 vols. ....*Warburton.*
——— Prince of Wales in ....*Woods.*
——— Winter Studies & Summer Rambles in, 3 vols. *Jameson.*
——— West, Twenty-seven years in, 2 vols. ......*Strickland.*
——— and the United States, Observations on ....*Grece.*
Canadas in 1841, 2 vols. ....*Bonnycastle.*
——— Travels through the, 4to. ....*Heriot.*
Canary Islands, History of, 4to. ....*Glas.*
Cancellor, R. C., Facts bearing on the Death of ......*Hopley.*
Canning, George, Memoirs of, 2 vols.
———— Poetical Works of
Canon of Scripture, Scholastical History of, 4to., 1683.

D

Canterbury Tales, modernized, 3 vols. ....*Chaucer.*
——————— modernized by Lee, 5 vols. .... ,,
——————— with Essay by Tyrwhitt, 5 vols. ... ,,
Cape of Good Hope, Journey from, 4to. ....*Reenen.*
——————— Notes on
——————— Voyage to, 2 vols., 4to. ......*Sparrman.*
Cape Kaffirs ....*Cole.*
Capefigue, M.—Diplomatists of Europe.
Capern, Thomas—Mesmerism, Curative Powers of
Capes, J. M.—A Sunday in London.
Capper, James—India through Egypt, Passage to, 4to.
Captain of the Vulture ....*Braddon.*
Carleton, Captain, Memoirs of
——— William—Irish Peasantry, Tales and Sketches of
Carew, Bamfylde Moore, Life and Adventures of
Caricature and Grotesque in Literature and Art ......*Wright.*
Carlen, Emilie —Matrimony, Twelve Months of
Carlisle, N.—Grammar Schools in England and Wales, 2 vols.
——— Earl of—Diary in Turkish and Greek Waters.
Carlyle, Thomas—Burns, Robert, Essay on
——————— Chartism.
——————— Essays, Critical and Miscellaneous, 4 vols.
——————— Frederick the Great of Prussia, 6 vols.
——————— French Revolution, History of, 3 vols.
——————— German Romance, 4 vols.
——————— Heroes and Hero Worship.
——————— Latter Day Pamphlets.
——————— Oliver Cromwell, Letters, &c. of, 3 vols.
——————— Past and Present.
——————— Sterling, John, Life of
Carmagnola; an Italian Tale.
Carnarvon, Earl of—Portugal and Galicia.
Carne, John—Letters from the East.
——————————— Switzerland and Italy.

Carne, John—Recollections of the East.
Caroline Matilda, Life and Times of ......*C. F. L. Wraxall.*
Carpenter, William B.—Alcoholic Liquors, Use and Abuse of
Carr, John—Baltic, Northern Summer Tour round, 4to.
————— Stranger in France, 4to.
————————— Ireland, 4to.
Carrington, R. C.—Sun, Observations of Spots on the
Carroll, Lewis—Alice's Adventures in Wonderland.
Carter, Edmund—Cambridge, County of, History of
————— Eliz. and Catherine Talbot, Letters between, 4 vols.
Cartwright, Dr. Edmund, Memoir of
Carver, Jonathan—America, Travels in North
Cary, John—Atlas of England and Wales, folio.
————— Traveller's Companion.
Case, Mrs.—Day by Day at Lucknow.
Casket, The; Unpublished Poems.
Castilian; a Poem ....*Talfourd.*
Castleacre, Castle and Priory at, History of ....*Bloom.*
Castle Dangerous ....*Scott.*
—— Rackrent ....*Edgeworth.*
—— Spectre and other Dramas ....*Lewis.*
—— of Otranto, 1791 ....*Walpole.*
Castles of Athlin and Dunbayne ....*Radcliffe.*
Catalogue of Royal & Noble Authors of England, 2 vols., 1757.
————— Great Exhibition, 1851.
————— (Official) of International Exhibition, 1862.
————— of Lansdowne MSS. in British Museum, folio.
————— Library of Rev. Samuel Parr.
Cathedrals of England, Northern, Handbook to, 2 vols....*King.*
————————————— Eastern,   ,, ... ,,
——————————— Southern,   ,,   2 vols.... ,,
——————————— Western,   ,, ... ,,
————— of Wales, Handbook to .... ,,
Catherine ....*Thackeray.*

D 2

Chatfield, Robert—Hindostan, Historical Review of, 4to.
Chatterton, Lady—Home Sketches, &c., 3 vols.
————— Ireland, Rambles in South of, 2 vols.
————— Pyrenees, with Excursions into Spain, 2 vols.
————— Thomas, Works of, 3 vols.
Chaucer, G.—Works of, folio, 1560.
————— Canterbury Tales, modernized, 3 vols.
—————————————————— by Lee, 5 vols.
—————————————— with Essay by Tyrwhitt, 5 vols.
————— Poems of, modernized by Wordsworth.
————— Life of, 2 vols., 4to. ....*Godwin.*
Chelsum, James—Remarks on last two Chapters of Gibbon.
Chemical Essays, 5 vols., 1787 ....*Watson..*
Chemistry, Treatise on ....*Donavan.*
————— Meteorology, &c. ....*Prout.*
————— Elements of, 2 vols., 4to., 1803 ....*Black.*
————————————— 4to., 1735 ....*Boerhaave.*
————— New Method of, 4to., 1727 ....*Shaw.*
————— Experimental, Institutes of, 2 vols., 1759 ...*Dosie.*
————— of Common Life, 2 vols. ....*Johnston.*
Cheselden, W.—Anatomy of Human Body, plates, 4to., 1740.
Chesney, Col.—Euphrates and Tigris, Expedition to, 2 vols.
Chesterfield, Earl of—Letters to his Son, 4 vols.
Chesterton, G. L.—Prison Life, Revelations of, 2 vols.
————— Peace, War, and Adventure, 2 vols.
Chief Justices, Lives of the, 3 vols. ....*Campbell.*
Child of the Islands ....*Norton.*
Childe Harold, 2 vols. ....*Byron.*
Children's Friend, 6 vols. ....*Berquin.*
Chili, Peru, and Brazil, Liberation of, 2 vols. ...*Dundonald.*
Chimes, The ....*Dickens.*
China, Campaign of, Closing Events in ....*Loch.*
——— Consular Cities of, Visit to ....*Smith.*
——— Embassy to, 4to. ....*Ellis.*

China, Embassy to, 3 vols. ....*Staunton.*
—— British Embassy to, 1792—1794 ....*Anderson.*
—— Dutch   ,,   2 vols. ....*Van Braam.*
—— Expedition to, 2 vols. ....*Bingham.*
—— Opened, 2 vols. ....*Gutzlaff.*
—— Report of Proceedings on a Voyage to ......*Lindsay.*
—— Tea Countries of, History of, 2 vols. ....*Fortune.*
—— Travels in, 4to. ....*Barrow.*
Chinese, The, 2 vols. ....*Davis.*
—— Expedition, Six Months with ....*Jocelyn.*
—— Residence among the ....*Fortune.*
Chips from a German Workshop, 2 vols. ....*Max Muller.*
Chirurgery, Introduction to, 1730 ....*Horne.*
Chirurgical Operations, 1699 ....*Vauguion.*
——— Works, 4 vols., 1771 ....*Potts.*
Chivalry, History of ....*James.*
Chorley, H. F.—Hemans, Felicia, Memorials of, 2 vols.
——— Music & Manners in France & Germany, 3 vols.
——— Thirty Years' Musical Recollections, 2 vols.
Chorographia Britanniæ, 1742.
Christ, Life of, 3 vols. ....*Strauss.*
—— of History ....*Young.*
—— Person and Atonement of ....*Urwick.*
Christ's Sermon on the Mount ....*Ogle.*
Christian and Turk, Frontier Lands of, 2 vols.
—— Art, Sketches of History of ....*Lindsay.*
—— Church, History of, 2 vols. ....*Stebbing.*
—— Doctrine, Treatise on, 4to. ....*Milton.*
——— and Practice in Second Century.
——- Hero ....*Steele.*
—— Morals ....*More.*
—— Religion, Essays on ....*Whateley.*
—— Researches in Asia ....*Buchanan.*
—— Revelation, Summary of ....*Beilby.*

Christian Revelation, Discourses on ....*Chalmers.*
———— Survey of the World ....*G. Penn.*
———— Year (36th edition) ....*Keble.*
Christian's Defence against the Fears of Death ...*Drelincourt.*
Christianity (translation from the French) ....*Coquerel.*
———— in Ceylon ....*Tennent.*
———— History of, 3 vols. ....*Milman.*
———— Influence of, on International Law ......*Kennedy.*
———— Inquiry into the Causes of Growth of ..*Dalrymple.*
———— Popular ....*Foxton.*
———— Practical, View of ....*Wilberforce.*
———— Reasonableness of ....*Locke.*
———— State of Man before Promulgation of
———— Latin, History of, 6 vols. ....*Milman.*
Christie Johnson ....*Reade.*
Christmas, Rev. Henry—The Phantom World, 2 vols.
———— Books ....*Dickens.*
———— ....*Thackeray.*
———— Carol ....*Dickens.*
———— Eve and Easter Day ....*Browning.*
Christopher Tadpole, Adventures of ....*Smith.*
Chronicles, 4to., 1811 ....*Rastell.*
———— of the Canongate, 2 series, 5 vols. ....*Scott.*
———— of England, France, & Spain, 12 vols. ...*Froissart.*
———— of Wolfert's Roost ....*Irving.*
———— and Characters, 2 vols. ....*Lytton.*
———— 6 vols., 4to., 1808 ....*Holinshed.*
———— 2 vols., 4to., 1809 ....*Grafton.*
———— 4to., 1809 ....*Halle.*
———— 4to., 1811 ....*Fabyan.*
———— 4to., 1812 ....*Hardyng.*
Chronology and History of the World, folio ....*Blair.*
———— of History ....*Nicolas.*
Chrysal, or Adventures of a Guinea, 1790.

Church, A. H.—Food, its Sources, Constituents, and Uses.
—— of Christ, History of, 4 vols. ....*Milner.*
———————————— 3 vols. ....*Stebbing.*
—— of the Future ....*Bunsen.*
—— Book of the, 2 vols. ....*Southey.*
—— Dictionary ....*Hook.*
—— of England, History of, 2 vols. ....*Short.*
—— of Scotland, ,, 2 vols. ....*Russell.*
———————— ,, 4to. ....*Kirkton.*
—— Eastern, Lectures on ....*Stanley.*
—— Jewish, Lectures on, 2 vols. .... ,,
Churches of Asia, Visit to the Seven ....*Arundell.*
Churchill, Charles, a Biographical Essay ....*Forster.*
———————— Poetical Works of, 2 vols.
Churchill's Collection of Voyages and Travels, 8 vols., folio.
Churchyard, Thomas—The Worthiness of Wales, 1776.
Chymical Essays, 2 vols , 1802 ....*Skrimshire.*
Cicero, M. T., Letters of, 3 vols., by Melmoth.
———————— Life of ....*Forsyth.*
———————— 2 vols. ....*Middleton.*
———————— Life and Letters of ...*Middleton and Melmoth.*
Cid, The, a Traji-Comedy, 1637.
Circassia, &c , Travels in, 2 vols. ....*Spencer.*
City of the Magyar, 3 vols. ....*Pardoe.*
—— Sultan, 2 vols. .... ,,
Civilization, History of, 2 vols. ....*Buckle.*
———— European, Lectures on ....*Guizot.*
Clairvoyance and Practical Mesmerism ....*Esdaile.*
Clapperton, Capt.—Africa, Second Expedition into, 4to.
——————————— Last Expedition, 2 vols. ..*Lander.*
Clare, John—Poems.
———— Shepherd's Calendar.
———— Village Minstrel and other Poems, 2 vols.
Clare Abbey ....*Ponsonby.*

Clarendon, Earl of—Rebellion in 1641, History of, 7 vols.

Clarissa Harlowe, 8 vols. ....*Richardson.*

Clark, Rev. T.—The Wandering Jew.

Clarke, Dr. Adam, Life and Labours of

———— Charles—Charlie Thornhill.

———— Mrs. Cowden—Concordance to Shakespeare.

———— Dr. E D., Life and Remains of, 4to.

——————— Travels of, 6 vols., 4to.

———— John Algernon—Fen Sketches.

———— W.—Connection of Roman, Saxon,& English Coins, 4to.

———— Zachary—Norfolk Charities, Account of

———— and McArthur—Nelson, Lord, Life of

Clarkson, Thomas—Antediluvian Researches.

——————— Penn, William, Life of, 2 vols.

——————— Quakerism, Portraiture of, 3 vols.

——————— Slave Trade, History of, 2 vols.

——————— Slavery, Essay on

——————— Wilberforce, Strictures on the Life of

Classical Instruction, with Interlinear Translation, viz , Æsop's Fables, Herodotus, Homer's Iliad, Lucian's Dialogues, Odes of Anacreon, Ovid's Metamorphoses, Xenophon's Memorabilia.

Clavis Calendaria ; Analysis of the Calendar, 2 vols. ...*Brady.*

Clayton, Helen C.—Queens of Song, 2 vols.

Clergymen, Amusements of ....*Stillingfleet.*

Cleveland, a Tale of the Catholic Church.

———— C. D.—Concordance to Milton's Poetical Works.

Clinical Medicine, Treatise on, 1827 ....*Bischoff.*

Clive, Lord, Life of, 3 vols. ....*Malcolm.*

Clockmaker, or Sayings of Sam Slick, 2 vols. ...*Halliburton.*

Closing Scene, The ....*Neale.*

Clough, Arthur H.—Poems.

Club Life of London, 2 vols. ....*Timbs.*

Clubs of London, 2 vols.

Clytemnestra, and other Poems ....*Lytton.*
Coalition, The, and France.
Cobbe, F. Power—Confessions of a Lost Dog.
Cobbett, William—Rural Rides.
———————— State Trials, 1163 to 1820, 34 vols.
Cochin China, Voyage to ....*White.*
Cochrane, Capt. J. D.—Russia & Tartary, Journey thro', 2 vols.
Cockburn, Lord—Jeffrey, Lord, Life of
———————— Memorials of His Time.
Cœlebs in Search of a Wife, 2 vols. ....*More.*
Cœur de Lion, a Poem, 2 vols. ....*Porden.*
Cogan, T.—Treatise on the Passions, 2 vols.
Coinage of Great Britain, 3 vols., 4to. ....*Ruding.*
——————— British Empire ....*Humphreys.*
Coins, Connection of Roman, Saxon, & English, 4to. ...*Clarke.*
———— Medals, and Gems, Essay on ....*Walsh.*
Coke, Sir Edward, Life of, 2 vols. ....*Johnson.*
Cole, Alfred W.—The Cape Kaffirs.
———— J. W.—Kean, Charles, Life and Times of, 2 vols.
Colenso, Bishop—The Pentateuch and Book of Joshua, 3 vols.
Coleridge, Rev. Derwent—On the Education of the People.
———————————— The Teachers of the People.
—————————————— Lay Sermons.
——————— Hartley—Essays and Marginalia, 2 vols.
———————·——— Poems, 2 vols.
——————— Mrs. H. N.—Phantasmion.
————————————— Shakespeare,Notes & Lectures on,2 vols.
———————— Samuel Taylor—Aids to Reflection.
———————————————— Biographia Literaria, 2 vols.
———————————————— Confessions of an Enquiring Spirit.
————————————— Dramatic Works of
————————————————— Essays on His Own Times, 3 vols.
—————————————— Friend, The, 3 vols.
————————·—————— Literary Remains, 2 vols.

Coleridge, Samuel Taylor—Poems.
——— ——————————— Poems on various Subjects.
————————————————— Poetical Works of, 3 vols.
—————————————— Poetical & Dramatic Works, 3 vols.
——————————————— Remorse, a Tragedy.
————— ——————————— Table Talk, Specimens of, 2 vols.
————————————————- Theory of Life.
——————— Sara—Pretty Lessons in Verse.
——————— Lamb, and Lloyd, Poems of, 1797.
——————— and Southey, Reminiscences of ....*Cottle.*
Coles, Thomas, Letters from and to ....*Foster.*
College Recollections.
Collegians, The, 3 vols. ....*Griffin.*
Collier, Sir George—France, Holland, &c., a Century Ago.
Collieries and Coal Trade.
Collingwood, Lord, Memoirs and Correspondence of, 4to.
Collins, C. A.—Cruise upon Wheels.
——————— The Eye Witness.
——————— New Sentimental Journey.
——————— At the Bar, 2 vols.
——— S.—Anatomy of Man & other Animals, 2 vols., fo., 1685.
——— Wilkie—Armadale, 2 vols.
——————— Basil.
——————— Hide and Seek, 3 vols.
——————— No Name, 3 vols.
——————— Plot in Private Life and other Tales.
——————— Woman in White.
——————— William, Life and Poetical Works of
Collinson, Rev. William—Thuanus, Life of
Colloquies on the Progress of Society, &c., 2 vols. ...*Southey.*
Colman, George—Prose on Several Occasions, 3 vols.
——————————— the younger—Broad Grins.
——— ——————————————— Poetical Vagaries.
Colonial Ecclesiastical Establishment ....*Buchanan,*

Confessions, &c. ....*Bury.*

———— of an Enquiring Spirit ....*Coleridge.*

———— of a Lost Dog ....*Cobbe.*

Congreve, William, Dramatic Works of

Conjugial Love ....*Swedenborg.*

Connection of Old & New Testaments, 2 vols., fo., 1718..*Prideaux.*

Connolly, T. W. J.—Romance of the Ranks, 2 vols.

Conolly, Lieut. A.—India, Travels to North of, 2 vols.

Conquest of England by the Normans, 3 vols. ......*Thierry.*

Consett, Matthew—Sweden, &c., Tour through, 4to.

Consolations in Travel ....*Davy.*

Constabulary Force Commissioners, First Report of

Constantinople, Ancient and Modern, 4to. ....*Dallaway.*

———— to England, Journey from ....*Walsh.*

———— Teheran, Journey from, 2 vols. ...*Fraser.*

———— Travels to and from, 2 vols. ......*Frankland.*

Constitution of Man ....*Combe.*

———— Moral, of Man, 2 vols. ....*Chalmers.*

———— of England ....*De Lolme.*

Contentment, The Way to

Continental Adventures, 3 vols.

Conversations on Some of the Old Poets ....*Lowell.*

———— Land and Water ....*Marcet.*

———— at Cambridge.

Conversion and Death of Count Struensee.

Convicts, Life among, 2 vols. ....*Gibson.*

Conybeare and Howson—St. Paul, Life and Epistles of, 2 vols.

———— Phillips—Geology of England and Wales.

Cook, Capt. Jas., Life of, 4to................................*Kippis.*

———— First Voyage, 3 vols., 4to.

———— Second Voyage, 1772-75, 2 vols., 4to.

———— Third Voyage, 1776-80, with Maps, 3 vols., 4to.

———— Narrative of, 2 vols. ...*Ellis.*

Cook, Modern ....*Francatelli.*

Coxe, Wm.—Marlborough, Duke of, Memoirs of, 6 vols. & Atlas.
————— Poland, Russia, &c., Travels into, 3 vols., 4to.
————— Walpole, Sir Robert, Memoirs of, 3 vols., 4to.
Crabbe, George, Poems of, 3 vols.
————— Poetical Works of
————— Tales of the Hall, 2 vols.
————— Works of, 5 vols.
————— Life of, by his Son.
Craik, Geo. L.—Pursuit of Knowledge under Difficulties, 2 vols.
————— Remarkable Trials, Reports of, vol. i.
————— Romance of the Peerage, 4 vols.
Cranford ....*Gaskell.*
Cranmer, Archbishop, Life of ....*Sargant.*
Crashaw, Richard—Steps to the Temple, 1648.
Craven, Lady—Crimea to Constantinople, Journey through
—— John J.—Davis, Jefferson, Prison Life of
—— R. K.—Naples, Tour through
Creasy, Edw. S.—Fifteen Decisive Battles of the World, 2 vols.
————— Eminent Etonians, Memoirs of
Creation, Works and Rest of the ....*Browne.*
Creed, Exposition of the, 1715, folio ....*Pearson.*
Crescent and the Cross, 2 vols. ....*Warburton.*
Cricket on the Hearth ....*Dickens.*
Crime, On ....*Hill.*
Crimea, Campaign in the ....*Woods.*
—— to Constantinople, Journey through ....*Craven.*
—— Invasion of the, History of, 6 vols. ....*Kinglake.*
—— Riga to, Journey from ....*Holderness.*
Critic, by Sheridan, and other Dramas.
Critick of Pure Reason, translated by Haywood ....*Kant.*
Crochet Castle, and other Tales.
Croker, J. W.—Guillotine, History of the
Croly, Rev. Geo.—George IV., Personal History of, 2 vols.
Cromek, R. H.—Reliques of Robert Burns.

E

Cromwell, Oliver, a Biographical Essay ....*Forster.*

———————— House of, Memoirs of, 2 vols. ....*Noble.*

———————— and His Times ....*T. Cromwell.*

———————— and Bunyan, Lives of ....*Southey.*

———————— Letters and Speeches of, 3 vols. ...*Carlyle.*

Cross, Robert—Physiology of Human Nature.

Crosthwaite's Maps, 1788.

Crowe, Catherine—Night Side of Nature.

———————— Spiritualism.

——— E. E.—France, History of, 3 vols.

———————————— Eminent Foreign Statesmen, 5 vols.

Croyland Abbey, Chronicle of ....*Ingulph.*

Cruden, Alexander—Concordance to Old and New Testaments.

Cruise of R. Y. S. Eva ....*Kavanagh.*

——— upon Wheels, 2 vols. ....*Collins.*

Crusaders, Tales of the, 4 vols. ....*Scott.*

Cudworth, Ralph—Intellectual System of the Universe.

Culinary Campaign ....*Soyer.*

Culloden Papers, 4to.

Cumberland, George—Original Tales, 2 vols.

——————— Richard—Calvary, a Poem, 2 vols.

————————————— Memoirs of, 4to.

Cumming, Dr. J.—The Great Tribulation.

——————— J. G.—Africa, A Hunter's Life in South, 2 vols.

——————— W. F.—A Wanderer in Search of Health, 2 vols.

Cumnor, or the Bugle Horn, a Tragedy ....*Impey.*

Cunningham, Allan—Wilkie, Sir David, Life of, 3 vols.

————————— Poems and Songs.

————————— Songs of Scotland, 4 vols.

———————— J. D.—Sikhs, History of the

———————— P.—New South Wales, Two Years in, 2 vols.

———————— Peter—London, Handbook of

Cureton, Wm.—Four Gospels, Ancient Syrian Recension of

Curiosities and Beauties of England displayed, fo. ...*Newman.*

Dancing Master (Music and Directions), 1721.

Danes & Norwegians in England, Scotland, & Ireland..*Worsaae.*

—— and Swedes ....*Scott.*

D'Anois, Countess—Fairy Tales, 2 vols., 1817.

Danube, Steam Voyage down the, 2 vols. ....*Quin.*

——— Mystery of the ....*Urquhart.*

Dante, A.—La Divina Commedia, translated by Boyd, 3 vols.

———————————————————— Cary, 3 vols.

———————————————————— Pollock.

D'Arblay, Madame, Diary and Letters of, 7 vols.

——————————— Burney, Dr., Memoirs of, 3 vols.

——————————— *See,* Burney, Frances.

Darien, or the Merchant Prince, 3 vols. ....*Warburton.*

Darley, George—Sylvia, or the May Queen.

Darwin, Chas.—Expression of the Emotions.

——————— Fertilization of Orchids.

——————— Geological Observations on Coral Reefs, &c.

——————— Journal of Researches into Natural History,&c.

——————— Naturalist's Voyage.

——————— Origin of Species.

——— Erasmus—Botanic Garden, 4to., 1791.

——————————— Memoirs of ....*Seward.*

——————————— Phytologia; Philosophy of Agriculture,4to.

——————————— Zoonomia, or Laws of Organic Life, 4 vols.

Daschkaw, Princess, Memoirs of, 2 vols.

Dasent, G. W.—Burnt Njal, Story of, 2 vols.

Dates, Dictionary of ....*Haydn.*

D'Aubigne, J. H. M.—Reformation of the 16th Century, 5 vols.

Daughters of England ....*Ellis.*

D'Aulnoy, Countess—Fairy Tales, translated by Planché.

Davenport Brothers, Biography of ....*Nichols.*

David Copperfield, 2 vols. ....*Dickens.*

Davidson, G. F.—Trade and Travel in the Far East.

Davies, David—Case of Labourers in Husbandry, 4to.

Davies, Thomas—Dramatic Miscellanies, 3 vols.

Davis, A. J.—Present Age and Inner Life.

——————— Principles of Nature and her Divine Revelations.

——— J. F.—The Chinese, 2 vols.

———Jefferson, Prison Life of ....*Craven.*

Davison, Sir William, Life of ....*Nicolas.*

Davy, Sir Humphrey—Agricultural Chemistry, 4to.

——————————— Consolations in Travel.

————————— ——— Memoirs of, 2 vols.

——— John—Ceylon, Travels in, 4to.

————— Ionian Isles and Malta, Notes, &c., on, 2 vols.

Dawbarn, William—Essays and Tales.

———————————— Government, Conduct, and Example.

Day, Thomas—Sandford and Merton.

————————— Life of

Dead Sea, Journey Round the, 2 vols. ....*De Saulcy.*

Death's Jest Book, or Fool's Tragedy, 1850.

Debates on the Grand Remonstrance ....*Forster.*

Decade of Italian Women, 2 vols. ....*Trollope.*

Decline and Fall of Nations, Inquiry into, 4to. ......*Playfair.*

Dee, Dr. John—Relation of his Action with Spirits, fo., 1659.

Deerbrook, 3 vols. ....*H. Martineau.*

Deer-Stalking, Art of ....*Scrope.*

De Foe, a Biographical Essay ....*Forster.*

——— Plague in London, 1665.

——— Robinson Crusoe, 2 vols., 1790.

Deformed, The

Delany, Mrs.—Letters to Mrs. Frances Hamilton.

Delmard, Sophia D.—Switzerland, Village Life in

De Lolme, J. L.—Constitution of England.

Democracy in America, 4 vols. ....*De Tocqueville.*

——————— France, 1849 ....*Guizot.*

Demonology and Witchcraft ....*Scott.*

Denham, Major D.—Africa, Travels and Discoveries in, 4to.

Diary of an Invalid ....*Matthews.*

—— of a late Physician ....*Warren.*

—— in Turkish and Greek Waters ....*Carlisle.*

—— or Woodfall's Register, 1791, folio.

Dibdin, Charles—Sea Songs and Ballads.

——————— Songs, illustrated by Cruikshank.

Dickens, Charles—American Notes, 2 vols.

——————— Barnaby Rudge, 2 vols.

——————— Battle of Life.

——————— Bleak House, 2 vols.

——————— Child's First History of England, 3 vols.

——————— Chimes, The

——————— Cricket on the Hearth.

——————— Christmas Books.

——————————— Carol.

——————— David Copperfield, 2 vols.

——————— Dombey and Son, 2 vols.

——————— Great Expectations.

——————— Grimaldi, Joseph, Memoirs of

——————— Hard Times.

——————— Haunted Man.

——————— Little Dorrit, 2 vols.

——————— Martin Chuzzlewit, 2 vols.

——————— Master Humphrey's Clock, 2 vols., 1840.

——————— Nicholas Nickleby, 2 vols.

——————— Old Curiosity Shop, 2 vols.

——————— Oliver Twist.

——————— Our Mutual Friend, 2 vols.

——————— Pickwick Papers, 2 vols.

——————— Pictures from Italy.

——————— Sketches by Boz, 2 vols.

——————— Tale of Two Cities.

——————— Uncommercial Traveller.

——————— Life of, 3 vols. ....*Forster*

Dictionary Appendix (published by Shaw).

———— Latin ....*Ainsworth.*

———— Classical ....*Lempriere.*

———————————— of the Vulgar Tongue ....*Grose.*

———— English, Etymological, 1736, folio ....*Bailey.*

———— of the English Language ....*Johnson.*

————————————————— ....*Webster.*

——————————————————— 4to. ....*Worcester.*

———— English and German ....*Flügel.*

———————————————— ....*Thïeme.*

————————————— Latin ....*Young.*

————— German and English ....*Meissner.*

———— Italian and English, 2 vols. ....*Baretti.*

———— of Greek and Roman Antiquities ...*Dr. W. Smith.*

———————————————————Biography, &c.   ,,   ,,

Dieffenbach, E.—New Zealand, Travels in, 2 vols.

Digby, K.—Morus; Disputations on Christian Chivalry, 1826.

Digestion, Physiology of ....*Combe.*

Dilke, C. W.—Greater Britain, 2 vols.

Dillenius, J. J.—Mosses & Corals, General History of, 4to.,1768.

Diplomatists of Europe ....*Capefigue.*

Dircks, Henry—The Ghost as produced in the Spectre Drama.

Directory, Cambrian

Discipline, 3 vols.

Discourses and Evening Thoughts ....*Burdett.*

———— bearing on the Controversy of the Day ......*Hook.*

Disowned, The, 3 vols. ....*Lytton.*

Dispensatory, The, 1720 ....*Bate.*

——————— Edinburgh, 1727 ....*Shaw.*

——————— English, 1733 ....*Alleyne.*

——————————— 1747 ....*James.*

——————————— 1726 ....*Quincy.*

————— of the Royal College of Physicians, 1727   ,,

—————— New, 1770.

Display, a Tale ....*Taylor.*
D'Israeli, Benj.—Bentinck, Lord Geo., a Political Biography.
———————— Henrietta Temple.
———————— Lothair.
——————— Sybil.
———————— Tancred.
———————— Vivian Grey, 5 vols.
———— Isaac—Amenities of Literature, 3 vols.
———————— Calamities of Authors, 2 vols.
———————— Curiosities of Literature, 2 series, 6 vols.
———————— Charles I., Commentaries on
———————— James I., Literary and Political Character of
———————— Literary Character, On, 2 vols.
——————————— Recreations.
———————— Men of Genius, 2 vols.
———————— Quarrels of Authors, 3 vols.
Dissertations, Moral and Critical, 4to. ....*Beattie.*
————————————— Literary ....*Percival.*
Diversions of Purley, 2 vols. ....*Tooke.*
Dixon, Hepworth—Free Russia, 2 vols.
———————— Holy Land, 2 vols.
———————— New America, 2 vols.
———————— Spiritual Wives, 2 vols.
———————— Switzers, 2 vols.
———— E. S.—Poultry, Ornamental and Domestic
Dobell, Peter—Kamtchatka and Siberia, Travels in, 2 vols.
Dobrizhoffer, M.—Abipones, Account of the, 3 vols.
Dobson, Susannah—Petrarch, Life of, 2 vols.
Doctor, The ....*Southey.*
———— Thorne ....*Trollope.*
Dod, C. R.—Peerage and Knightage, 1864, 1867, 2 vols.
Doddridge, Dr. P.—Sermons, 4 vols.
———————— Passages in the Life of Col. Gardiner.
Dods, J. B.—Philosophy of Electrical Psychology.

Dodsley, J.—Collection of Poems, 6 vols., 1782.
———— Fugitive Pieces, 1771.
Dolomite Mountains ....*Gilbert and Churchill.*
Dombey and Son, 2 vols.
Domesday Book, 4 vols., folio.
———————— translated by Bawdwen, 4to.
———————— Illustrated ....*Kelham.*
Domestic Anecdotes of the French Nation.
———— Economy ....*Donavan.*
——————————— of Great Britain and Ireland ...*Chalmers.*
———— Liturgy ....*Dale.*
Domus Carthusiana ; Account of Charter House, 1677 ...*Herne.*
Donaldson, J. W.—The New Cratylus.
Donavan, Michael—Chemistry, Treatise on
——————— Domestic Economy.
Don Carlos and other Plays ....*Schiller.*
——Juan ....*Byron.*
——Quixote, 2 vols. ....*Cervantes.*
Doran, Dr.—Monarchs Retired from Business, 2 vols.
Dorsey, Anna H.—Woodreve Manor.
Dosie,[—].—Experimental Chemistry,Institutes of,2 vols.,1759.
Douglas, James—Lateral Operation, History of, 4to., 1726.
————Sir Howard—Naval Gunnery, Treatise on
Dover, Lord—Frederick the Great, Life of, 2 vols.
Downey, Thomas—Naval Poems, 4to.
D'Oyly, George—Archbishop Sancroft, Life of, 2 vols.
Do you give it up ? (Conundrums).
Drafts on My Memory, 2 vols. ....*Lennox.*
Drakard, John—Stamford, History of
Drake, Jas.—Anatomy, New System of, plates, 3 vols., 1727.
Drake, Nathan—Essays, illustrative of the Tatler, &c., 4 vols.
———————— Evenings in Autumn, 2 vols.
———————— Literary Hours.
———————— Mornings in Spring, 2 vols.

Drake, Nathan—Noontide Leisure, 2 vols.

———————— Winter Nights, 2 vols.

——— Sir F., Life and Voyages of ....*Barrow.*

Dramas ....*Sir W. Scott.*

——— Sacred ....*H. More.*

——— 3 vols. ....*Baillie.*

Dramatic Art and Literature, Lectures on, 2 vols. ...*Schlegel.*

——— Miscellanies, 3 vols. ....*Davies.*

——— Table Talk, 3 vols. ....*Ryan.*

——— Works ....*Coleridge.*

————————— ....*Farquhar.*

———————— 3 vols. ....*Knowles.*

——— and Political Works ....*Baillie.*

Dramatis Personæ; Poems ......ᴧ...................*R. Browning.*

Drayton, Michael—Polyolbion, small folio, 1613.

Dream, The, and other Poems ....*Mrs. Norton.*

——— of Life, and other Poems ....*Moultrie.*

Dred, a Tale of the Dismal Swamp, 2 vols. ....*Stowe.*

Drelincourt, Chas.—Christian's Defence against Fears of Death.

Drinkwater, John—Gibraltar, History of Siege of, 4to.

Drummond, James L.—Letters to a Young Naturalist.

———————— William, Poems of

Dryden, John, Life of ....*Scott.*

———————— Works of, 18 vols., edited by Scott.

Duality of the Mind ....*Wigan.*

Du Broca, M.—Heroic Women, Anecdotes of

— Chaillu, P. B.—Africa, Explorations in Equatorial

———————— Ashango Land, Journey to

Dudley, Earl of—Letters to the Bishop of Llandaff.

——— Robert, Earl of Leicester, Secret Memoirs of, 1706.

—————————————————— Life of, 1727.

Dufferin, Lord—Letters from High Latitudes.

Dugdale, Sir William, Life of, 4to.

Dulwich College, Catalogue of Pictures in (pamphlet) *Bourgeois.*

Dumas, Alexander—Celebrated Crimes.

———————— History of a Nutcracker, 2 parts.

Dumont, Etienne—Recollections of Mirabeau.

Dundonald, Earl of—Chili, Peru, & Brazil, Liberation of, 2 vols.

———————— Agriculture & Chemistry, Connection, 4to.

———————— Autobiography of a Seaman.

Dunham, S. A.—Germanic Empire, History of, 3 vols.

Dunster, Charles—Early Reading of Milton.

Dunton, John, Life and Errors of, 2 vols.

Dupin, Baron—Commercial Power of Great Britain, 2 vols.

Duppa, R.—Michael Angelo, Life of

Dupuis, Joseph—Ashantee, Residence in, 4to.

Dura Den, a Monograph of the Yellow Sandstone ...*Anderson.*

Durer, Albert--The Artist's Married Life.

Dutch Republic, Rise of the, 3 vols. ....*Motley.*

Duties of Men, Enquiry into, 2 vols. ....*Gisborne.*

———— Women, ,, ... ,,

Dutton, Francis—South Australia and its Mines.

Dwight, Timothy—New England, &c., Travels in, 4 vols.

Dyer, George—Cambridge University, History of, 2 vols.

———————————————— Privileges of, 2 vols.

———————— Robinson, Robert, Life of

—— Thomas H.—Pompeii, its History and Antiquities.

Dynamics of Magnetism, Electricity, &c. ....*Reichenbach.*

EARL, G. W.—Voyages in the Eastern Seas.

Early Lessons, or Stories for Children, 4 vols. ...*Edgeworth.*

—— Start in Life ....*Norris.*

Earth, Inquiry into the Original State of, 4to. ...*Whitehurst.*

———— Theory of the ....*Cuvier.*

———————————— 1725 ....*Whiston.*

Earthly Paradise, 4 vols. ....*Morris.*

East, Travels in the, 4to. ....*Walpole.*

—— Anglia, Vocabulary of, 2 vols. ....*Forby.*

Elgin Marbles, Report on the
—— James, the 8th Earl of, Letters & Journals of ... *Walrond.*
Elia, Essays of, 2 vols. ....*Lamb.*
Eliot, George—Middlemarch.
——————— Silas Marner.
——————— Spanish Gypsy.
—— Sir John ; a Biography, 2 vols. ....*Forster.*
—— Samuel—The Liberty of Rome.
—— W. G.—Portugal, The Defence of
Elizabeth, Court of, Memoirs of, 2 vols. ....*Aikin.*
————— Proceedings in Chancery in Reign of, 4 vols., folio.
————— or the Exiles of Siberia ....*Cottin.*
Ellen Middleton ....*Fullerton.*
Elliotson, Dr. J.—Human Physiology.
——————— State Medicine, Lectures on
——————— Prussic Acid, Report on
——————— Mesmeric State, Surgical Operations in
Elliott, Chas. B.—Austria, Russia, & Turkey, Travels in, 2 vols.
——————— North of Europe, Letters from
Ellis, Hy.—China, Embassy to, 4to.
————— F.R.S.—Letters illustrative of English Hist., 2 vols.
—— Mrs.—Daughters of England.
————— Wives of England.
————— Women of ,,
————— Summer and Winter in the Pyrenees.
—— Rev. William—Hawaii, Tour through
——————— Madagascar, History of, 2 vols.
——————— Revisited.
——————— Three Visits to
——————— Polynesian Researches, 2 vols.
——————— Life of ....*J. E. Ellis.*
—— W.—Narrative of Cook's Voyage, 1776—1780, 2 vols.
Elmes, James—Wren, Sir Christopher, Memoirs of, 4to.
Elmhirst, P. J.—Calabria Ulteriore, Six Months' Residence in

England, History of, Abridged, to 1858.

———————————————— by Sadler ....*Lingard.*

——————————— Child's First, 3 vols. ....*Dickens.*

——————————— Constitutional, 2 vols. ....*Hallam.*

————— Old and New ....*Bunn.*

————— View of, 2 vols. ....*Wendeborn.*

———— in 1835, 3 vols. ....*Raumer.*

————— Eastern, 2 vols. ....*White.*

————— and Scotland, History of Union of ....*Marshall.*

————————————— Travels in, 2 vols. ....*Saint Fond.*

————————————— in 1785, Tour in

————— and Wales, Beauties of, 26 vols.

————— Wales, & Scotland, Travels through, 2 vols. ...*Spiker.*

English at Home, 2 vols. ....*A. Esquiros.*

————— in Italy, 3 vols.

————— History, Cameos from, Rollo to Edward II. ...*Yonge.*

——————————— Letters illustrative of, 7 vols. ....*Ellis.*

——————————— Synopsis of ....*Grimaldi.*

————— Bards and Scotch Reviewers ....*Byron.*

————— Composition, Principles of ....*Booth.*

————— Eccentrics and Eccentricities, 2 vols. ....*Timbs.*

———— Fashionables Abroad, 3 vols.

————— Government and Constitution, History of ...*Russell.*

————— Hermit, or Adventures of Philip Quarll.

————— Life in the Middle of the 19th Century.

————— Lyrics ....*Smyth.*

————— Manners, Brief Remarks on

————— Merchants, 2 vols. ....*Bourne.*

————— Past and Present ....*Trench.*

————— Travellers and Italian Brigands, 2 vols. ......*Moens.*

Englishwomen of Letters, 2 vols. ....*Kavanagh.*

Ennemoser, Joseph—Magic, History of

Enoch Arden ....*Tennyson.*

Enterprising Impresario ....*Maynard.*

F

Exodus Papyri, The ....*Heath.*
Exposition of the 51st Psalm (title wanting).
Expository Notes on the Acts & Epistles, fo., 1703 ...*Burkitt.*
Eye Witness, The ....*Collins.*
Eyre, Lieut. V.—Afghanistan, Journal of Imprisonment in
—— Edward J.—Australia, Discoveries in Central, 2 vols.
—— Mary—A Lady's Walks in the South of France.

FABER, Rev. G. S.—On the Prophecies, 3 vols.
——— M.—France, Sketches of the Internal State of
Fable of the Bees ; or Private Vices and Public Benefits.
Fables of Æsop with Reflections, folio, 1694.
Fabyan, Robert—Chronicles of England and France, 1811.
Facts, A Million of ....*Phillips.*
—— Failures, and Frauds ....*Evans.*
Faggot of French Sticks, 2 vols.
Fair Maid of Perth ....*Scott.*
Fairholme, George—Geology of Scripture.
Fairy Tales, 2 vols., 1817 ....*D'Anois.*
——— translated by Planché ....*D'Aulnoy.*
Falconer, W.—Natural History, Tracts relative to, 4to., 1793.
——— William—The Shipwreck, a Poem.
Falconry in the Valley of the Indus ....*Burton.*
Family Records ....*Bury.*
—— Romance, 2 vols. ....*Burke.*
Fancourt, Charles St. John—Yucatan, History of
Fancy, The ....*Corcoran.*
Fanny Hervey.
Fanshawe, Lady, Memoirs of
Farce of Life ....*Lord B——*
Farm, Our, of Four Acres, and the Money we made by it.
Farmer, Henry—Miracles, Dissertation on the
Farquhar, George—Dramatic Works of
Fatal Revenge, 3 vols.

Feuerbach, A. von—Kaspar Hauser, Account of
Fevers, Mechanical Account of, 1720 ....*Bellini.*
Fichte, J. G.—Vocation of Man.
———— ———— ———— the Scholar.
———— ——— Nature of the Scholar.
———— ———— Way towards the Blessed Life.
Fiction, Noted Names of, Dictionary of ....*Wheeler.*
Field, B.—New South Wales, Memoirs on
—— Rev. William—Parr, Dr. Samuel, Memoirs of, 2 vols.
—— Sports of North of Europe, 2 vols. ....*Lloyd.*
Fielding, Henry—Tom Jones, 3 vols., 1780.
———— ———— Works of, 10 vols.
Fiends, Ghosts, and Sprites ....*Radcliffe.*
Finati, Giovanni, Life and Adventures of, 2 vols.
Fine Arts, Letters on the...............................*H. Milton.*
Fireside Book, 1829 ....*Tayler.*
First Season, My
Fisher, Alexander—Parry's Voyage, Journal of
Fishes, British, History of, 3 vols. .... *Yarrell.*
———— Amphibians, and Reptiles, 2 vols. ....*Swainson.*
Fisk, Rev. G.—Holy Land, A Pastor's Memorial of
Fitzadam, A.—The World, 4 vols.
Fitzgerald, Lord Edward, Life of, 2 vols. .... *Moore.*
Five Years of Youth ....*H. Martineau.*
Flagellants, History of the
Fleming, John—Zoology, Philosophy of, 2 vols.
Fletcher, Rev. J. P.—Nineveh, Two Years' Residence at, 2 vols.
———— James—Poland, History of
Flirtation, 3 vols. .... *Bury.*
Flodden Field, Battle of, a Poem ....*Weber.*
Flora Cantabrigiensis ....*Relhan.*
—— Londinensis, vol. i., folio ....*Curtis.*
Florence Macarthy, 4 vols. ....*Morgan.*
———— Commonwealth of, History of ....*Trollope.*

Forster, John—Arrest of the Five Members.
——————— Biographical Essays.
——————— Debates on the Grand Remonstrance.
——————— Defoe and Churchill, Lives of
——————— Dickens, Charles, Life of, 3 vols.
——————— Eliot, Sir John, a Biography, 2 vols.
——————— Goldsmith, Oliver, Life of, 2 vols.
——————— Historical and Biographical Essays, 2 vols.
——————— Jebb, Bishop, Life of, 2 vols.
——————— Statesmen of the Commonwealth, 5 vols.
—————— T.—The Perennial Calendar.
Forsyth, Joseph—Italy, Antiquities, &c., of, Remarks on
—————— J. S.—Antiquary's Portfolio, 2 vols.
—————— William—Fruit and Forest Trees, Treatise on
——————— M.A.—Cicero, Life of
——————————-- Napoleon, Captivity of
Fort Montague at Knaresborough, Account of, pamphlet.
Fortune, Robert—Tea Countries of China, 2 vols.
——————— Chinese, Residence among the
Fortunes of Nigel, 3 vols. ....*Scott.*
——————— the Scattergood Family ....*Smith.*
Forty Days in the Desert ....*Bartlett.*
Fosbrooke, T. D.—Antiquities, Encyclopædia of, 2 vols., 4to.
——————— British Monachism, 4to.
——————— Foreign Topography, 4to.
——————— Monastic Life, Economy of, 4to.
Foss, Edw.—Grandeur of the Law, or Legal Peers of England.
Fossil Insects, History of ....*Brodie.*
Foster, John—Essays to a Friend, 2 vols.
—————— Popular Ignorance, Essay on
—————— Letters to and from Thomas Coles.
Fotheringay, Historic Notices of ....*Bonney.*
Four Ages, The ....*Jackson.*
—— Georges, The ....*Thackeray.*

France, before the Revolution of 1798, Society in .*De Tocqueville.*
——— South of, A Lady's Walks in ....*Eyre.*
——— Middle Classes, Monarchy of, 2 vols. ....*Bulwer.*
——— Restoration of the Monarchy in, 4 vols. ...*Lamartine.*
——— Reformed Religion in, 3 vols. ....*Smedley.*
——— History of, during Reign of Napoleon, 7 vols.
——— Eminent Men of, 2 vols.
——— Men and Women of, during Last Century.
——— Holland, &c., a Century Ago ....*Collier.*
——— and Italy, Society and Manners in, 4 vols. ...*Moore.*
——— Italy, and Germany, Maps of
——— and Russia, Sketches on the Intrinsic Strength of, 4to.
——— Savoy, &c., Tour in, 2 vols. ....*Stevenson.*
Francis I., Life and Times of, 2 vols.
Frank, 3 vols. ....*Edgeworth.*
——— Fairlegh ....*Smedley.*
Frankland, C. C.—Russia and Sweden, Courts of, 2 vols.
——————— Constantinople, Travels to and from, 2 vols.
Franklin, Benjamin—Life and Essays of, 2 vols.
————————————— Writings of, 6 vols.
————— Sir John—Polar Sea, Journey to, 4to.
———————————— Second Journey to, 4to.
———————————— 1st and 2nd Journeys to, 4 vols.
————————— A Summer Search for ....*Inglefield.*
————————— Grinnell Expedition in Search of ...*Kane.*
————————— The Prince Albert in search of ...*Kennedy.*
————————— Discovery of the Fate of ...*Mc Clintock.*
————————— Career and Fate of ....*Osborn.*
————— William—Camarupa and Camalata, Loves of
Fraser, J. B.—Constantinople to Teheran, Journey from, 2 vols.
Frederick the Great—History of His Own Times, 13 vols.
——————— Life of, 6 vols. ....*Carlyle.*
——————————— 2 vols. ....*Dover.*
——————————— Anecdotes of

Fuller, Thomas—Worthies of England.
Fullerton, Lady G.—Ellen Middleton.
———————————— Grantley Manor.
Fullom, F. W.—Marvels of Science.
Furioso, or Passages from the Life of Beethoven.
Furley, Robert—Weald of Kent, History of, 3 vols.
Fuseli, Henry—Painting, Lectures on, 4to.
———————— Life and Writings of, 3 vols. ....*Knowles.*

GAFFAREL, James—Horoscope, Curiosities of the, 1650.
Gainsborough, Thomas, Life of ....*Fulcher.*
Galignani's Paris Guide.
Galleries of Portraits with Memoirs, 7 vols.
Gallus, translated by Rev. F. Metcalfe ....*Becker.*
Galt, John—Literary Life and Miscellanies of, 3 vols.
———————— West, Benjamin, Life of, 2 vols.
———————— Wolsey, Life and Administration of
Galton, Francis—Trophical South Africa.
Gamba, Count—Byron's Last Journey to Greece, 2 vols.
Gambado, Geoffrey—Academy for Grown Horseman, 4to..1787 .
Garcilasso de la Vega—Works of, by Wiffen.
Garden, My, its Plan and Culture ....*Smee.*
Gardener's Calendar, or Practical Gardener ....*Mawe.*
Gardening, Encyclopædia of ....*Loudon.*
Gardens and Menagerie of the Zoological Society, 2 vols.
Gardenstone, Lord—Travelling Memoranda, 1786-88, 2 vols .
Gardiner, Colonel, Passages in Life of ....*Doddridge.*
Garibaldi, Joseph, an Autobiography .. ..*Dumas.*
Garnet, M., Trial and Execution of, 1606.
Garnett, T.—Annals of Philosophy, 2 vols.
Garratt, G.—Instinct, Marvels and Mysteries of
Garrick, David, Poetical Works of, 2 vols.
———————— Life of, 2 vols. ....*Murphy.*
Gaskell, Mrs.—Brontë, Charlotte, Life of, 2 vols.

Gaskell, Mrs.—Cranford.

——————— Grey Woman, and other Tales.

————————— Mary Barton, 2 vols.

——————— Ruth, 3 vols.

Gaslight and Daylight ....*Sala.*

Gaston de Blondeville, 4 vols. ....*Radcliffe.*

Gay, John, Poetical Works of

—————————— and Dramatic Works of, 6 vols.

Gazetteer, General, abridged, 1796 ....*Brookes.*

——————— of France, 3 vols.

——————— of Netherlands.

Gell, Sir Wm.—Rome and its Vicinity, Topography of, 2 vols.

Gem, The, edited by Hood.

Gems and Jewels, their History, &c. ....*Barrera.*

Genii, Tales of the, 2 vols. ....*Ridley.*

Genth, Adolphus—Mineral Waters of Schwalbach.

Gentz, Fredk.—Europe before and after French Revolution.

Gentle Gertrude ....*Kelty.*

——————— Life ....*Friswell.*

Gentleman of the Old School ....*James.*

Gentleman's Magazine, 1796 to 1798, 3 vols.

————————————— 1868 to 1882.

Geoffrey Crayon—*See*, Irving, Washington.

Geoffroy, S. F.—Substances used in Physic, 1736.

Geographical Description of the World, folio, 1670 ...*Blome.*

Geography, Encyclopædia of, 1844 ....*Murray.*

——————— Grammar of ....*Goldsmith.*

—— ——— Physical, Principles of ....*Malte Brun.*

——————— History of the Rise of ....*Blair.*

——————— Modern, System of ....*Guthrie.*

—————— Universal, System of ......*Malte Brun and Balbi.*

——— ——— and History, Handbook of Ancient ....*Putz.*

——————— of Cities and Towns of the World.

Geological Evidences of the Antiquity of Man ....*Lyell.*

Germania; Courts, Camps, and Peoples, 2 vols. ......*Bury.*
Germanic Empire, History of, 3 vols. ....*Dunham.*
Germany, 3 vols. ....*De Staël.*
——— in 1831, 2 vols. ....*Strang.*
——— History of ....*Markham.*
——— Revolutions of the Empire of ....*Butler.*
——— Tour in
——————————— ....*Semple.*
——— Travels through, 3 vols. ....*Riesbeck.*
——— Notes during a Ramble in
——— Visit to, 2 vols. ....*Faulkner.*
——— Rural and Domestic Life in ....*Howitt.*
——— Student's Life in .... ,,
——— Bohemia, &c., in 1837, 3 vols. ....*Gleig.*
——— France, &c., Rambles in, 1842-3, 2 vols. *Mrs. Shelley.*
——— Sweden, Russia, &c., Tour in, 4to. ....*James.*
Gertrude of Wyoming, and other Poems, 4to. ......*Campbell.*
Gesta Romanorum, or Moral Stories, 2 vols. ....*Swan.*
Ghost as produced in the Spectre Drama ....*Dircks.*
—— Seer, The ....*Schiller.*
—— Stories ....*Jarvis.*
Giants' Causeway, Guide to the ....*Wright.*
Giaour, The ....*Byron.*
Gibbon, Edward—Roman Empire, Decline and Fall of, 8 vols.
———————————————— abridged by Dr. Wm Smith.
————————— Letters to ....*Travis.*
————————— Miscellaneous Works, 2 vols., 4to.
————————— Remarks on Last Two Chapters of..*Chelsum.*
Gibraltar, Siege of, 4to. ....*Drinkwater.*
Gibson, Charles—Life among Convicts, 2 vols.
—— Thomas—Anatomy, 1703.
Giffard, Edward—Ionian Islands, Athens, &c., Visit to
Gifford, William—Baviad and Mæviad.
Gil Blas, 4 vols. ....*Le Sage.*

Gilbert Gurney, 3 vols.

———— Limney—Nature and Science, Beauties & Wonders of

———— and Churchill—The Dolomite Mountains.

Gilfillan, George—Gallery of Literary Portraits.

Gillespie, Major General, Memoirs of

Gillies, R. P.—German Stories, 3 vols.

Gilly, Wm. S.—Felix Neff, Memoirs of

————————— Waldensian Researches in Piedmont, 2 vols.

——— W. O. S.—Shipwrecks of the Royal Navy.

Gilpin, William—Dialogues on Various Subjects.

———————— Hampshire, Observations on the Coast of

Gillray, James, Caricatures of, Account of ...*Wright & Evans.*

Gisborne, Thomas—Enquiry into the Duties of Men, 2 vols.

——— ———— ———— ———— ———— ——— Women.

———————— Moral Philosophy, 2 vols.

———————— Poems of

Gisippus, a Play ....*Griffin.*

Glaisher, James—Travels in the Air.

Glanville,J.—Witches&Apparitions,Evidence concerning,1726.

Glas, George—Canary Islands, History of, 4to.

Glaucus, or the Wonders of the Sea Shore ....*Kingsley.*

Gleanings from Pious Authors ....*J. Montgomery.*

——— through Wales, Holland, &c., 6 vols. ....*Pratt.*

Gleig, G. R.—British Military Commanders, 3 vols.

——————— Germany, Bohemia, &c., in 1837, 3 vols.

——————— Hastings, Warren, Memoirs of, 3 vols.

——————— Munro, Sir Thomas, Life of, 3 vols.

——————— Sale's Brigade in Afghanistan.

——————— Waterloo, Story of the Battle of

Glencoe, and other Poems ....*Talfourd.*

Glossary, Provincial, of Local Proverbs ....*Grose.*

Gobat, Rev. Sam.—Abyssinia, Three Years' Residence in

God, Attributes of, 3 vols. ....*Macculloch.*

——— and Man ....*R. Montgomery.*

G

God's Revenge against Murder, 1640 ....*Reynolds.*
Godolphin, 3 vols. ....*Lytton.*
————— Mrs., Life of ....*Evelyn.*
Godwin, Wm.--Caleb Williams, 3 vols.
————— ——— Chaucer, Life of, 2 vols., 4to.
————— ——— Commonwealth of England, History of, 4 vols.
————— ——— Mandeville, a Tale of 17th Century, 3 vols.
————— ——— Orphans of Unwalden.
————— ——— St. Leon, 4 vols.
Goëthe, J.—Autobiography, 2 vols.
————— Conversations of, with Eckerman & Soret, 2 vols.
————— Faust, translated by Talbot.
————— ——— &c., translated by Lord Gower.
————— Novels and Tales.
————— Sorrows of Werter.
————— Wilhelm Meister's Apprenticeship, 3 vols.
————— Life and Works of, 2 vols. ....*Lewes.*
————— Memoirs of, 2 vols.
Golberry, S. M. X.—Africa, Travels in, 2 vols.
Gold Digger, The, pamphlet ....*Mackenzie.*
Golden Legend, The ....*Longfellow.*
————— Sceptre, The, 1638 ....*Preston.*
Goldsmith, Lewis—Bonaparte, Secret History of the Cabinet of
————— Oliver—Animated Nature, History of, 8 vols.
————— ——— England, History of
————— ——— Greece,   ,,
————— ——— Rome,   ,,
————— ——— Geography, Grammar of
————— ——— Vicar of Wakefield.
————— ——— Works of, 4 vols.
————— ——— Life of, 2 vols. ....*Prior.*
————— ——— ——— ....*Forster.*
Golownin, Capt.—Japan, Captivity in, 2 vols.
————— ——— and the Japanese, 2 vols.

Grammar, Short Introduction to, 1787.
——— Eton Greek .. ..*Wright.*
——— Schools, Endowed, in Eng. & Wales, 2 vols. *Carlisle.*
Granada, Conquest of, 2 vols. ....*Irving.*
Granby, 3 vols.
Grandeur of the Law, or Legal Peers of England ... . *Foss.*
Grandison, Sir Charles, History of, 7 vols. ......*Richardson.*
Grant, James—Origin of Society, &c., Essays on, 4to.
——— Mrs.—Superstition of the Highlanders, 2 vols.
————— Letters from the Mountains, 2 vols.
Grantham, Collections for the History of ....*Turnor.*
Grantley Manor ....*Fullerton.*
Granville, A. B.—St. Petersburg, Travels to and from, 2 vols.
-——————— Spas of Germany, 2 vols.
——————————— England, 3 vols.
——— George—Poems on Several Occasions, 1726.
——— Mary, Autobiography of, 2 series, 6 vols.
Gratton, Henry, Life and Times of, 5 vols.
——— T. C.—Netherlands, History of
Gravel and Stone, Treatise on the, 1723 ....*Robinson.*
Graver Thoughts of a Country Parson ....*A. K. H. Boyd.*
Gray, Mrs. Hamilton—Etruria, Sepulchres of
-—— Thomas—Poems and Letters.
——— ——— Life and Poems.
——— ——— and Mason, Wm., Correspondence of..*Mitford.*
Grazier, The Complete
Great Britain, History of, 2 vols. ....*Belsham.*
——————————— 6 vols., 4to. ....*Henry.*
——— ——— ——— ——— continuation of, vol. i. ...*Andrews.*
——— ——— in 1833, 2 vols. ....*D'Haussez.*
——————— Tour in, by a Frenchman, 2 vols.
——————— Climate of .. ..*Williams.*
——————— Commercial Power of, 2 vols. ....*Dupin.*
——————— Foreign Affairs of, Survey of ....*Leckie.*

Grey, Hon. C.—Prince Consort, Early Years of
—— Sir George—Polynesian Mythology.
—— Capt. Geo.—Australia, Discoveries in, 2 vols.
———————————————— Travels in N.W. and W., 2 vols.
—— Hon. Mrs. William—Egypt, &c., Journal of a Visit to
—— Woman, and other Tales ....*Gaskell.*
Greyson, R. E. H.—Selections from Correspondence of
Griffin, Gerald—The Collegians, 3 vols.
——————— Gisippus, a Play.
——— R.—Trades, Book of
Griffith Gaunt, 3 vols. .... *Reade.*
——— Thomas—A Present for the Afflicted.
Grimaldi, Stacey—English History, Synopsis of
———— Joseph, Memoirs of ....*Dickens.*
Grimshawe, T. S.—Richmond, Rev. Legh, Memoir of
Gronow, Capt.—Celebrities of London and Paris.
————— Last Recollections of
————— Recollections and Anecdotes.
————— Reminiscences of
Grose, Francis—Classical Dictionary of Vulgar Tongue.
————— Provincial Glossary of Local Proverbs.
Grossmith, William R., the Juvenile Actor, Life of
Grote, George—Greece, History of, 12 vols.
Gryll-Grange.
Guardian, The, edited by Alex. Chalmers, 2 vols.
Guesses at Truth, 2 series ....*A. and J. Hare.*
Guicciardini, Fran.—Italy, History of, 1490—1532, 10 vols.
Guide to Chatsworth, pamphlet.
—— Hampton Court, pamphlet.
—— Hayling Island, Hants.
—— the Lakes of Cumberland.
—— Liverpool, pamphlet.
—— Leamington, ,,
—— Lowestoft, ,,

Guide through Peak's Hole, Castleton, pamphlet.
Guido and Lita, fcap. 4to. ....*Marquis of Lorne.*
Guillemin, Amédée—The Forces of Nature.
Guillotine, History of the ....*Croker.*
Guizot, Madame—Popular Tales.
—— F. P. G.—Civilization, European, Lectures on
———————— Democracy in France, 1849.
———————— Embassy to the Court of St. James in 1840.
———————— Peel, Sir Robert, Memoirs of
———————— Revolution of England in 1649.
———————— Washington, Life & Character of, Essay on
Gulliver's Travels, 2 vols. ....*Swift.*
Gurney, Joseph J.—Prisons, Notes on
———————— West Indies, Winter in
—— Married, 3 vols., sequel to Gilbert Gurney.
Gurwood, John—Wellington, Dispatches & Orders of, 13 vols.
Gushington, Hon. Impulsia—Lispings from Low Latitudes.
Gustavus Adolphus, and the Thirty Years' War ...*Chapman.*
———————— Life of, 2 vols. ....*Harte.*
———— IV., Last Years of the Reign of
Guthrie, William—Modern Geography, System of, 4to.
Gutzlaff, Rev. Charles—China Opened, 2 vols.
Guy Livingstone.
——Mannering ....*Scott.*
Gypsies, Dissertation on the, 4to. ....*Raper.*
—— in Spain, Zincali or ....*Borrow.*

H—— Family, The ....*Bremer.*
Habershon, Dr.—Diseases of the Stomach.
Hackett, Bishop—Century of Sermons, folio, 1765.
Hahn-Hahn, Countess—Faustina.
———————— Ulrich, a Tale.
Half-Hours with the Best Authors, 4 vols. ....*Knight.*
—— Sisters ....*Jewsbury.*

Halford, Sir Henry—Essays and Orations.

Haliburton, T.C.—The Attaché, or Sam Slick in England, 2 vols.

———————— Clockmaker, or Sayings of Sam Slick, 3 vols.

Hall, Capt. Basil—America, North, Travels in, 3 vols.

———————— American Station, South, 1820-22, 2 vols.

———————— Patchwork, 3 vols.

———————— Schloss Hainfeld, a Winter in Lower Styria.

———————— Voyages, Fragments of, 3 series, 9 vols.

—— Capt. C. F.—Life with the Esquimaux, 2 vols.

—— Robert—Memoir of ....*Gregory.*

—— Mr. and Mrs. S. C.—Ireland, its Scenery, &c., 3 vols.

Hallam, Arthur H.—Remains in Prose and Verse.

———— Henry—England, Constitutional History of, 2 vols.

———————— Europe, State of, during Middle Ages, 3 vols.

———————— Supplemental Notes to ditto.

———————— Literature of Europe, 1400—1700, 4 vols.

Halle, Edward—Chronicles, 4to., 1809.

Haller, Albert—Physiology, Lectures on, 2 vols.

Halliday, Andrew—Savage Club Papers for 1868.

Halls, J. J.—Salt, Henry, Life and Correspondence of, 2 vols.

Hamilton, Elizabeth—Education, Letters on

———— James—Africa, Wanderings in North

———— Rev. James—Life in Earnest.

———————— Mount of Olives.

Hampshire, Observations on the Coast of ....*Gilpin.*

Hand, The, as evincing Design ....*Bell.*

—— Phrenologically Considered.

—— of God in History ....*Read.*

Handbook of Essex, Suffolk, Norfolk, Cambs., 1870...*Murray.*

———————— Europe, Northern, 3 vols., 1849 .... ,,

———————— France, 1858 .... ,,

———————— Germany, Northern, 1865 .... ,,

———————————— Southern, 1851 .... ,,

———————— Italy, Central, and Rome, 1850 .... ,,

Handbook of Sardinia, Lombardy, & Venice, 1856 ...*Murray.*

———— Tuscany and Florence, 1856 .... ,,

Hanger, Col. G., Life and Opinions of, 2 vols.

Hankinson, Thomas E.—Poems.

———————— Sermons.

Hanmer, Sir John—Fra Cipolla, and other Poems.

Hanna, Dr.—Chalmers, Dr. Thomas, Memoirs of, 4 vols.

Hard Times ....*Dickens.*

——— with Pictures from Italy .... ,,

Hardcastle, Ephraim—Twenty-ninth of May, 2 vols.

——————— Wine and Walnuts, 2 vols.

Hardy, Francis—Charlemont, Earl of, Life of, 2 vols.

——— Lieut.—Mexico, Travels in Interior of

Hardyng, John—Chronicles, 4to., 1812.

Hare, Archdeacon—Mission of the Comforter.

—— Augustus and Julius—Guesses at Truth, 2 series.

————— J. C.—Memorials of a Quiet Life, 2 vols.

Harleian Miscellany, 10 vols., 4to.

————— Selections from, 4to.

Harold, 3 vols. ....*Lytton.*

Harrington and Ormond, 3 vols. ....*Edgeworth*

Harris, John—The Pre-Adamite Earth.

——— W. C.—Æthiopia, Highlands of, 3 vols.

———— Wild Sports of Southern Africa.

——— Rev. John—Mammon.

Harry and Lucy, 4 vols. ....*Edgeworth.*

Harte, Walter—Gustavus Adolphus, Life of, 2 vols.

Hartley, David—Man, Observations on, 3 vols.

Hartshorne, Rev.C.H.—Book Rarities in Cambridge University.

Harvey, Mrs.—Turkish Harems and Circassian Homes.

Hastings, Warren, Memoirs of, 3 vols. ....*Gleig.*

——————— Simpkin the Second's Letter on the Trial of

Haunted London ....*Thornbury.*

——— Man ....*Dickens.*

Haussez, Baron d'—Great Britain in 1833, 2 vols.
Havelock, Hy.—Afghanistan, Narrative of the War in, 2 vols.
Hawaii, Tour through ....*Ellis.*
Haweis, Rev. H. R.—Ashes to Ashes.
———————— Music and Morals.
Hawkesworth, John—Voyages Round the World, 4 vols.
Hawkins, Sir John—Probationary Odes for the Laureateship.
———— Letitia M.—Anecdotes & Biographical Sketches, vol. i.
Hawthorne, Nathaniel—Blythedale Romance, 2 vols.
———————— House of Seven Gables.
———————— Mosses from an Old Manse.
———————— Scarlet Letter.
———————— Transformation, 3 vols.
———————— Twice Told Tales, 2 vols.
———————— Tales, 2 vols., containing :—
　　　　(1) Twice Told Tales, Snow Image, &c.
　　　　(2) House with Seven Gables, Scarlet Letter.
Hay, J. H. Drummond—Western Barbary, Wild Tribes of
Haydn, Joseph—Dictionary of Dates.
———— and Mozart, Lives of
Haydon, Benjamin Robert, Life of ....*Taylor.*
———— Robert, Autobiography of, 3 vols.
———— and Hazlitt—Painting and the Fine Arts.
Hayley, Wm.—Cowper, Wm., Life and Writings of, 4 vols.
———————— Plays, 4to.
———————— Poems, 4to.
———————— 6 vols., 1785.
———————— Memoirs of, 2 vols., 4to.
Hayward, A.—Diaries of a Lady of Quality, 1797—1844.
Hazlitt, William—Human Action, Essays on Principles of
———————— Spirit of the Age.
———————— Table Talk, or Original Essays, 2 vols.
Head, Sir F. B.—Emigrant, The
———————— Ireland, Fortnight in

Hogg, J. T.—Shelley, P. B., Life of, 2 vols.

Holcroft, Thomas—Tales of the Castle, 5 vols.

——————— Hugh Trevor, Adventures of, 6 vols.

Holderness, Mary—Riga to the Crimea, Journey from

Holdich, Benjamin—Weeds of Agriculture, pamphlet.

Holford, Miss—Wallace, a Metrical Romance.

Holidays with Hobgoblins ....*Costello.*

Holinshed, R.—Chronicles, 6 vols., 4to., 1808.

Holland, Reflections on the Government of, 3 vols. *L. Bonaparte.*

—————— Sir Henry—Ionian Islands, Travels in, 4to.

——————————— Mental Physiology, Chapters on

——————————— Recollections of a Past Life.

—————— House, 2 vols. ....*Liechtenstein.*

—————— Lord—Foreign Reminiscences.

Holliday, John—William, Earl of Mansfield, Life of, 4to.

Hollingshead, John—Odd Journeys.

————————— Under Bow Bells.

————————— Underground London.

Holman, James—Voyages and Travels, 4 vols.

Holmes, Oliver Wendell—Elsie Venner.

Holy Land, 2 vols. ....*Dixon.*

————— A Pastor's Memorial of the ....*Fisk.*

————— Letters on the, 2 vols. ....*Lindsay.*

————— Pilgrimage to the, 3 vols. ....*Lamartine.*

————— Tour in, Journal of ....*Egerton.*

Holyrood, Court of

Home Sketches & Foreign Recollections, 3 vols. ...*Chatterton.*

—— Thrusts, or Raps at the Rappers.

—— D. D.—Incidents in My Life.

—— John, Life of ....*Mackenzie.*

——————— Rebellion in 1745, History of, 4to.

Homer, Iliad of, translated by Pope, 6 vols.

————————————————— Earl Derby, 2 vols.

Homes of the New World, 3 vols. ....*Bremer.*

Homes and Haunts of British Poets, 2 vols. ....*Howitt.*
——— without Hands ....*Wood.*
Homilies with Various Readings.
Hood, Thomas—Comic Annual, 1830 to 1835, 1837 and 1838.
——————— Gem, The
——————— Memorials of, 2 vols.
——————— National Tales, 2 vols.
——————— Poems.
——————— Whims and Oddities.
——————— Wit and Humour.
——————— the Younger—Pen and Pencil Pictures.
——————————————— and others—Bunch of Keys.
Hook, Theodore E.—Cousin Geoffrey & Claude Stocq, 3 vols.
——————— Jack Brag, 3 vols.
——————— Parson's Daughter, 3 vols.
——————— Life and Remains of, 2 vols. ...*Barham.*
——————— A Sketch.
——— Dean—Archbishops of Canterbury, Lives of, 5 vols.
———— Discourses on the Controversies of the Day.
———— Church Dictionary.
Hooke, Nathaniel—Roman History, 11 vols.
Hooker, Richard, Works of, folio, 1682.
——— Joseph D.—Himalayan Journals, 2 vols.
——— & Taylor—Muscologia Britannica; Mosses of Britain.
Hooper, Lieut. W. H.—Tuski, Ten Months among Tents of the
Hop o' My Thumb, illustrated by Cruikshank.
Hope, Dr. James, Memoir of
——— Thomas—Architecture, Essay on, 2 vols.
——————— Anastasius, or Memoirs of a Greek, 3 vols.
Hopley, Thomas—Cancellor, R. C., Facts bearing on Death of
Horace, Odes of, translated by Francis.
———————————————— Boscawen.
——————— Latin and English, 4 vols. ....*Francis.*
——— in London.

H

Howitt, Wm. & Mary—Literature & Romance of N. Europe.
Hoyle's Games.
Huber, M. P.—Ants, Natural History of
——— Francis—Bees, ,, ,,
Huc, M.—Thibet and China, Travels in
Hudibras, 1775 ....*Butler.*
Hudson and Kennedy—Mont Blanc, Ascent of
Hudson's Bay to Northern Ocean, Journey from, 4to. *Hearne.*
Hugh Trevor, Adventures of, 6 vols. ....*Holcroft.*
Hughes, Rev. James—Bibliolatry, an Essay.
——— Thomas—Tom Brown's School Days.
——— Rev. T. S.—England, History of, 1760 to 1837, 7 vols.
————————— Greece, Travels in, 2 vols.
——— William—Australian Colonies.
Hugo, Thomas—The Bewick Collector.
Huguenots, History of the ....*Browning.*
Huish, Robert—Bees, The Management of
Hull, History of, 4to. ....*Frost.*
Human Action, Principles of, Essays on ....*Hazlitt.*
——— Hair practically & physiologically considered. *Rowland.*
——— Knowledge, On, 1734 ....*Berkeley.*
——— Life .... *Rogers.*
————— Illustrations of, 3 vols.
——— Nature, Inquiries into, 1680 ....*Charleton.*
——— Progression, Theory of
——— Understanding, Essay on ....*Locke.*
Humboldt, A. von—America, Ancient Institutions of, 2 vols.
————————— Cosmos, 3 vols.
————————— Letters to Varnhagen von Ense.
————————— New Spain, Political Essay on, 4 vols.
————————— Narrative of Travels, vols. i., ii., v., vi., vii.
Hume, David—England, History of, to 1688, 8 vols.
————— Essays and Treatises, 2 vols.
Humphreys, H. N.—Coinage of the British Empire.

99

Humphreys, W. N.—Shakespeare, Sentiments and Similies of
Hungary, Personal Adventures during the War in ...*Von Beck*.
———— My Life and Acts in, 1848, 1849 ....*Görgei*.
———— War of Independence in, Memoir of ......*Klapka*.
———— and Transylvania, 2 vols. ....*Paget*.
Hunt, F. K.—Fourth Estate, The, 2 vols.
—— John-—Age of Bronze.
—— Leigh—Byron and His Contemporaries, 2 vols.
———— Correspondence of, 2 vols.
———— Feast of the Poets, &c.
———— Foliage, Poems Original and Translated.
———— Men, Women, and Books, 2 vols.
———— Poetical Works of
———— Stories from the Italian Poets.
———— Autobiography of, 3 vols.
—— Robert—Poetry of Science.
———— Great Exhibition of 1861, Synopsis of
Hunter, Dr. J., F.R.S.—Human Teeth, Natural History of, 4to.
—— John D.—Indians, Captivity among the
—— Joseph—Diary of Ralph Thoresby, 2 vols.
Hunting in Africa ....*Baldwin*.
—— Grounds of the World, Adventures on ......*Meunier*.
Huntingdon, History of
Hurdis, Rev. James—Favourite Village, &c.
Hursthouse, C.—New Zealand, the Britain of the South, 2 vols.
Hussar, The, 2 vols.
Hutchesson, Mann—Wisbech, Introduction to Charter of, 4to.
———— Scarborough, Journal of a Tour to
Hutchinson, Colonel, Memoirs of
———— Francis—Witchcraft, Historical Essay on, 1718.
Hutton, William—Bosworth Field, Battle of
———— Derby, History of
———— Life of
Hydrostatics and Pneumatics ....*Lardner*.

H 2

Hymns for Little Children.

Hypatia, 2 vols. ....*Kingsley.*

Hyperion ....*Longfellow.*

IBBETSON, Capt.—Geology of the Isle of Wight.

Iceland, Journal of a Residence in, 2 vols, ...*Henderson.*

———— Journey to, & Travels in Norway & Sweden ...*Pfeiffer.*

———— Travels in, 4to. ....*Mackenzie.*

Idler, 2 vols. ....*Johnson.*

—— in France, 2 vols.   ....*Blessington.*

—— in Italy, 3 vols.   ....   ,,

Idylls of the King ....*Tennyson.*

Illustrated London News, 1842 to 1857, 23 vols.

——————————————— Queen's Visit to Germany in 1845.

Imagination, Tales of the ....*Poe.*

Imitation of Christ ....*T. à Kempis.*

Impey, E. B.—Cumnor, or the Bugle Horn, a Tragedy.

Imposture, Deception, and Credulity, Sketches of

Improvisatore, The ....*Andersen.*

Inchbald, Mrs.—Farces, Collection of, 7 vols.

——————— British Theatre, 25 vols.

——————— Modern Theatre, 10 vols.

——————— Nature and Art, 2 vols.

——————— A Simple Story, 4 vols.

Incidents in My Life ....*Home.*

Incubi of Rome and Venice ....*Beggi.*

India, History of, 2 vols. ....*Elphinstone.*

—— Historical Disquisition on, 4to. ....*Robertson.*

—— Observations on the Egyptian Passage to, 4to....*Capper.*

—— Excursions in, 2 vols. ....*Skinner.*

—— Sketches of, 1811—1814.

——————— by an Officer.

—— Six Years in, 3 vols. ....*Mackenzie.*

—— English Interests in, View of ....*Fullarton.*

India, Overland Journey to, 2 vols. ....*Elwood.*
—— Journey to, 2 vols. ....*Skinner.*
—— to England, Journey from ....*Jackson.*
———————————————————— 4to. ....*Keppel.*
—— Sepoy War in, History of, 3 vols. ....*Kaye.*
—— North of, Travels to, 2 vols. ....*Conolly.*
—— Upper Provinces of, Journey through, 2 vols., 4to. *Heber.*
—— Central, Memoir of, 2 vols. ....*Malcolm.*
—— Ceylon, &c., Voyages and Travels to, 3 vols. ...*Valentia.*
——————————— Plates to above, 4to.
Indian Recreations, vol. iii. ....*Tennant.*
Indians, Captivity among the ....*Hunter.*
—— North American, Manners & Customs of, 2 vols. *Catlin.*
Indies, East and West, History of, 8 vols. ....*Raynal.*
—— West, Six Months in, in 1825.
——————— Winter in ....*Gurney.*
——————— and the Spanish Main ....*Trollope.*
Indigence, Treatise on ....*Colquhoun.*
Industrial Biography ....*Smiles.*
Infant Education, The Importance of ....*Wilderspin.*
Infirmities of Genius, 2 vols. ....*Madden.*
Ingelow, Jean—Poems.
——————— Story of Doom, and other Poems.
Inglefield, E. A.—Franklin, Sir J., Summer Search for
Inglis, Henry D.—Channel Islands.
——————— Ireland in 1834, 2 vols.
——————— Spain in 1830, 2 vols.
——————— Switzerland and South of France.
——————— Tyrol, 2 vols.
Ingoldsby Legends, 3 vols. ....*Barham.*
Ingram, Rev. James—Oxford, Memorials of, 3 vols.
Ingulph's Chronicle of the Abbey of Croyland.
Inheritance, The, 3 vols. ....*Ferrier.*
Initials, The, 3 vols.

Italy in 1841, Visit to, 2 vols. ....*Trollope.*
—— Travels through, 4 vols. ....*Kotzebue.*
—— Tour through ....*Martyn.*
—— Classical Tour through, 2 vols., 4to. ....*Eustace.*
—— Journal of a Residence in, 3 vols. ....*Morgan.*
—— Ancient Manners in, Vestiges of ....*Blunt.*
—— Antiquities of, Remarks on ....*Forsyth.*
—— and the Italians, 2 vols. ....*Raumer.*
—— &c., Eminent Men of, 3 vols.
———— Tour in ....*Tobin.*
—— Spain and Portugal ....*Beckford.*
———————————— with Vathek .... ,,
—— and Sicily, Tour in ....*Simond.*
——————— Classical Tour through, 2 vols. ......*Hoare.*
Italian, The, 3 vols. ....*Radcliffe.*
—— Poets, the Early ....*Rossetti.*
—— Republics, History of the ....*Sismondi.*
Iu-Kiao-Li, or Two Fair Cousins, 2 vols.
Ivan at Home, or Pictures of Russian Life ....*Barry.*
Ivanhoe ....*Scott.*

JACK Brag, 3 vols. ....*Hook.*
—— and the Bean Stalk, illustrated by Cruikshank.
Jackson, James G.—Marocco, Empire of, Account of, 4to.
——————— Timbuctoo and Housa, Account of
—— Jeremiah—Horæ Subsecivæ, Wisbech Charities, &c.
—— John—India to England, Journey from
—— Dr. Thomas, Works of, vol. i., folio, 1653.
—— William—The Four Ages.
Jacob (Patriarch), Lectures on ....*Blunt.*
—— William—Precious Metals, On the, 2 vols.
———— Spain, Travels in South of, 4to.
Jacobinism, History of, 4 vols. ....*Barruel.*
Jacobite Memoirs of the Rebellion of 1745 ....*Chambers.*

Jesse, J. H.—Pretenders, Lives of the, 2 vols.

——— ——— Selwyn, George, and his Contemporaries, 4 vols.

—— Capt. William—Russia and the War.

Jest Book ....*M. Lemon.*

Jesuits, Fall of the, History of ....*De Saint Priest.*

Jews, A Few Words to the

—— Antiquities of the, 2 vols. ....*Brown.*

—— History of the, 3 vols. ....*Milman.*

Jewish Church, History of, 2 vols. ....*Stanley.*

Jewsbury, G. E.—The Half Sisters.

Joan of Arc, a Poem ....*Southey.*

Job, Book of, with Annotations by Randolph ......*E. Smith.*

Jocelyn, Lord—Chinese Expedition, Six Months with

Joe Miller's Jests.

Johnson, Charles—Fern Allies, parts i.—v.

——— James—Recess, a Tour to the Highlands.

——— Cuthbert Wm.—Coke, Sir Edward, Life of, 2 vols.

——— Samuel—Dictionary of the English Language.

——————— English Poets, Lives of the, 4 vols.

——————— Hebrides, Journey to the

——————— Idler, 2 vols.

——————— Rambler, 4 vols., 1793.

——————— Rasselas.

——————— Works of, 12 vols.

——————— Miscellaneous and Fugitive Pieces, 3 vols.

——————— Poems and Life, edited by F. M. Blagdon.

——————— Letters to and from, 2 vols. ...*Mrs. Piozzi.*

——————— Life of, 2 vols., 4to. ....*Boswell.*

——————————— 5 vols. (Croker's edition) ,,

——————— Life and Genius of, Essay on ...*Murphy.*

————————————— Writings of, Essay on ...*Towers.*

Johnston, James F. W.—Chemistry of Common Life, 2 vols.

——— A. Keith—Atlas, Royal Handy, 1868.

——— William—England as it is, 1851.

Kennedy, Wm.—Sir J. Franklin, Second Voyage in Search of

Kent, Edward Duke of, Life of ....*Neale.*

Kentish Kings, Pedigree of ....*Jenkins.*

Keppel, George—Balcan, Journey across the, 2 vols.

———————— India to England, Journey from, 4to.

———— Henry—Borneo, Expedition to, 2 vols.

———— Admiral, Life of

Khivah, Russian Expedition agst., trans. by Morier. *Zimmerman.*

Khondistan, The Wild Tribes of ....*Campbell.*

Kickleburys on the Rhine ....*Thackeray.*

Kidd, John—On the Physical Condition of Man.

King Arthur ....*Lytton.*

———— Edw.—Morsels of Criticism on N. T., 2 vols., 4to., 1788.

———— Lord—Locke, John, Life of

———————— Selections from Speeches and Writings of

———— P. J. L.—Law of Succession to Real Property of Intestates.

———— R. J.—Cathedrals of Eng. & Wales, Handbooks to, 7 vols.

———— Rev. Robert J., Memoir of ....*Watson.*

Kingdom of Christ ....*Whateley.*

Kinglake, Alexander W.—Crimea, Invasion of, 5 vols.

———————— William—Eothen, a Narrative of Eastern Travel.

King's Lynn, Navigation of, History of, 1725 ......*Armstrong.*

———— Own ....*Marryat.*

Kingsley, Charles—Alton Locke, 2 vols.

———————— Andromeda, and other Poems.

———————— Glaucus, or Wonders of Sea Shore.

———————— Hypatia, 2 vols.

———————— Two Years Ago.

———————— Westward Ho !

———————— Yeast, a Problem.

———————— Junr.—Saints' Tragedy.

Kinneir, J. M.—Persian Empire, Geographical Memoir of, 4to.

Kippis, A.—Biographia Britannica, vols. i.—v., folio.

———— Capt. Cook, Life of, 4to.

Lamb, Charles—Rosamund Gray and Old Blind Margaret.

——— Pattrick—Cookery Book, 1710.

Lambert, John—America, Travels in, 3 vols.

Lament of Tasso ....*Byron.*

Lamia, Isabella, and Eve of St. Agnes ....*Keats.*

Lancelot, Dom. C.—Alet and La Grande Chartreuse, 2 vols.

——— F.—Australia as it is.

Land of the North Wind ....*Rae.*

Landed Gentry, History of, 5 vols., 1848 ....*Burke.*

——— Dictionary of, 3 vols., 1852 .... ,,

Lander, R.—Africa, Clapperton's Last Expedition into, 2 vols.

——— R. and J.—Niger Expedition, Journal of, 3 vols.

Landor, Walter S.—Last Fruit Off an Old Tree.

——— Works of, 2 vols.

Landon, L. E.—Poetical Works of, 4 vols.

——— Romance and Reality.

Lands of the Messiah, Mahomet, and the Pope, 2 vols....*Aiton.*

Lane, E. W.—Ancient Egyptians, Manners & Customs, 2 vols.

Lang, J. D.—Australian Emigrant's Manual.

Language, Lectures on the Science of, 2 vols. ...*Max Müller.*

Lankester, Dr. E.—Food, Lectures on

Lanzi, A. L.—Painting in Italy, History of, 6 vols.

La Perouse, Voyage in Search of, 2 vols. ......*Labillardiere.*

——— of, Round the World, 3 vols.

Lapland and Sweden, Winter in, 4to. ....*Brooke.*

——— Tour in, 2 vols. ....*Linnæus.*

Lara and Jacqueline ....*Byron.*

Lardner, Dr. Dion.—Arithmetic.

——— Astronomy, Popular

——— Common Things Explained.

——— Electricity and Magnetism, 2 vols.

——— Geometry, Treatise on

——— Heat, Treatise on

——— Hydrostatics and Pneumatics.

I

Le Sage, A. R.—Gil Blas, 4 vols.
Leslie, Charles R.—Autobiographical Recollections, 2 vols.
Letter to a Friend ....*Lindsay.*
Letters from Abroad, 2 vols. ... .*Sedgwick.*
———— the Baltic, 2 vols.
———— the East ....*Carne.*
———— England, 3 vols. ....*Espriella.*
———— High Latitudes ....*Dufferin.*
———— Italy, 2 vols. ....*Miller.*
———————— North of, 2 vols. ....*Rose.*
———— Hofwyl on De Fellenberg's Institutions.
———— Madras, and Negro Life in West Indies.
———— Portugal, Spain, &c. ....*Broughton.*
———— the South, 2 vols. ....*Campbell.*
———— to Napoleon, intercepted between Paris and Dresden.
———— a Philosophical Unbeliever, 2 vols., 1787.
———— Varnhagen von Ense ....*Humboldt.*
———— a Young Lady, 3 vols. ....*West.*
———— a Young Man, 3 vols. .... „
Lettice Arnold.
———— I.—Scotland, Tour through, in 1792.
Le Vaillant, M.—Africa, Travels in, 2 vols.
———————————— New Travels in, 3 vols.
Levant, Tour in the, 3 vols. ....*Turner.*
Lewes, George Henry—Goëthe, Life and Works of, 2 vols.
Lewis, M. G.—Castle Spectre, and other Dramas.
———— The Monk, 3 vols.
———— Romantic Tales.
———— Tales of Wonder, and other Poems.
———— Lady T.—Semi-detached House.
———— and Clarke—America, Travels in
Lexicon, Greek ....*Liddell and Scott.*
Leyden, John—Africa, Discoveries and Travels in, 2 vols.
———— Life and Poetical Remains of

Literary Recollections, 2 vols. ....*Warner.*
——— Recreations ....*I. D'Israeli.*
Literature, Amenities of, 3 vols. .... ,,
——— Curiosities of, 2 series, 6 vols. .... ,,
——— Letters on ....*Heron.*
——— Varieties of, 2 vols.
——— of Europe from 15th to 17th centuries, 4 vols. *Hallam.*
——— of the South of Europe, 4 vols. ....*Sismondi.*
——— English, Sketches of, 2 vols. ......*Chateaubriand.*
——— Bibliographer's Manual of, 6 vols. *Lowndes.*
——— and Romance of Northern Europe. *W. & M. Howitt.*
Little, Thomas—Poetical Works of
———Dorrit, 2 vols. ....*Dickens.*
Livery Companies of London, The Twelve (incomplete) *Herbert.*
Livingstone, D.—Africa, Last Journals in Central, 2 vols.
——— Missionary Labours in South
——— Search after ....*Young.*
——— D. and C.—Zambesi and its Tributaries.
Livy, T.—Rome, History of, 6 vols., by Baker.
Lizzie Leigh and other Tales.
Lloyd, L.—Field Sports of the North of Europe, 2 vols.
———H. E.—Alexander I. of Russia, Life of
Loch, G. G.—China, Campaign of, Closing Events in
——— James—Improvements on Lord Stafford's Estates.
Locke, John—Christianity, Reasonableness of
——— Human Understanding, Essay on, 2 vols.
——— Understanding, Conduct of the
——— Witchcraft, History of, 2 vols.
——— Works of, 9 vols.
——— Life of ....*King.*
Lockhart, J. G.—Scott, Sir W., Memoirs of, 7 vols.
——— Spanish Ballads.
Lodge, E.—Peerage of British Empire, 1834.
Logan, James—The Scottish Gael, 2 vols.

Loseley Manuscripts, &c., Henry VIII. to James I. ...*Kempe.*

Lost Senses, The, (Deafness and Blindness), 2 vols. ...*Kitto.*

—— Tales of Miletus ....*Lytton.*

Lothair ....*B. D'Israeli.*

Loudon, J. C.—Arboretum Britannicum, 8 vols.

———————— Agriculture, Encyclopædia of

———————— Gardening, ,,

———————— Plants, ,,

Louis XIV., Life and Times of, 4 vols. ....*James.*

—— XV., Private Life of, 4 vols. ....*Justamond.*

—— XVI., Correspondence of, 3 vols. ....*Williams.*

———————— Last Years of, 3 vols. ....*Moleville.*

—— XVII., Life of, 2 vols. ....*Beauchesne.*

—— Philippe, Life and Times of ....*Wright.*

—— Prince of Condé, Life of ....*Mahon.*

—— Napoleon, Letters of an Englishman on

Lounger, The, 3 vols.

Lounger's Common Place Book.

Love me little, Love me long ....*Reade.*

—— Story, A ....*Southey.*

Loves of the Angels ....*Moore.*

Lowell, J. R.—Conversations on Some of the Old Poets.

Lower, M. A.—English Surnames, Essays on

Lowndes, W. F.—Bibliographer's Manual, 6 vols.

Luc, J. A. de—Physical Theory of the Earth, Letters on

Luciad, The, an Epic Poem, translated by Mickle, 4to. *Camoens.*

Lucian, Works of, 4 vols., translated by Francklin.

Lucile ....*R. Lytton.*

Lucknow, Siege of, Narrative of ....*Rees.*

———— Day by Day at ....*Case.*

Lucretia, 3 vols. ....*Lytton.*

Lucubrations of Humphrey Ravelin.

Lumley, Benjamin—Reminiscences of the Opera.

Lushington, Mrs. C.—Calcutta to Europe, Journey from

Luther, Martin, Boyhood of

———————— Life of ....*Michelet.*

Lux Renata, a Protestant's Epistle, pamphlet.

Lycia, Discoveries in ....*Fellows.*

Lyell, Sir Charles—Geological Evidences of Antiquity of Man.

——————— Geology, Principles of, 3 vols.

——————— America, Travels in North, 2 vols.

——————— United States, Second Visit to, 2 vols.

Lyndhurst and Brougham, Lords, Lives of ....*Campbell.*

Lyndsay, Margaret, Trials of ....*Wilson.*

Lynn, Navigation of, History of, folio, 1725 ......*Armstrong.*

—— History of, 2 vols. ....*Richards.*

Lyon, G. F.—Arctic Regions, Journal of H.M.S. Hecla in

Lyre of David, translation ....*Bythner.*

Lyrical Ballads, and other Poems, 2 vols. ......*Wordsworth.*

Lysons, D.—Cambridgeshire, Topographical Account of, 4to.

———————— London, Environs of, 5 vols., 4to.

Lytton, Sir E. B.—Alice, or the Mysteries, 3 vols.

——————— Caxtons, 3 vols.

——————— Devereux, 3 vols.

——————— Disowned, 3 vols.

——————— Ernest Maltravers, 3 vols.

——————— Eugene Aram, 3 vols.

——————— Godolphin, 3 vols.

——————— Harold, 3 vols.

——————— King Arthur, a Poem.

——————— Last of the Barons, 3 vols.

———————— Days of Pompeii, 3 vols.

——————— Lost Tales of Miletus.

——————— Lucretia, 3 vols.

——————— My Novel, 4 vols.

——————— Night and Morning, 3 vols.

——————— Not so bad as we seem, a Comedy.

——————— Paul Clifford, 3 vols.

Lytton, Sir E. B.—Pelham, 3 vols.
——————— Pilgrims of the Rhine, illustrated.
——————— Poetical and Dramatic Works.
——————— Rienzi, 3 vols.
——————— Siamese Twins, a Satirical Poem.
——————— Strange Story, 2 vols.
——————— Student, 2 vols.
——————— Tales and Poems.
——————— What will he do with it? 4 vols.
——————— Zanoni, 3 vols.
——— Lady—The World and his Wife, 3 vols.
——— R. Bulwer—Chronicles and Characters, 2 vols.
——————— Clytemnestra and other Poems.
——————— Lucile.
——————— Ring of Amasis, 2 vols.
——————— Serbski Pesme; National Songs of Servia.
——————— Wanderer, The

MACAULAY, Lord—Addison and Walpole, Lives of
——————— England, History of, 5 vols.
——————— Essays, Critical and Historical.
——————— Lays of Ancient Rome.
——————— Miscellaneous Works of, 2 vols.
——————— Speeches of
MacCann, W.—Argentine Provinces, 2000 miles ride thro', 2 vols.
Macculloch, John—Western Islands of Scotland, 2 vols.
——————— Plates to above, 4to.
——————— Highlands and Islands of Scotland, 4 vols.
——————— Attributes of God, 3 vols.
Macdiarmid, John—National Defence, System of, 2 vols.
Macdonnell, Count—Diary of an Austrian Secretary of Legation.
Macfarlane, Charles—Romance of History, Italy, 3 vols.
Macgregor, J.—Rob Roy Canoe on the Baltic.
——————————————— Jordan.

Macgregor, J.—Rob Roy Canoe, A Thousand Miles in the
Macilwain, George—Abernethy John, Memoir of, 2 vols.
Macirone, F.—Murat, Joachim, Fall and Death of
Mackay, Chas.—Legendary and Romantic Ballads of Scotland.
———— —— Popular Delusions, Extraordinary, 2 vols.
———— —— Thames and its Tributaries.
—— Alexander—Western World in 1846—7.
—— William—Intellect, Progress of the
Mackenzie, Rev. D.—The Gold Digger, pamphlet.
—— Henry—Home, John, Life of
———— —— Julia de Roubigné, 2 vols.
———— —— Man of Feeling.
———— —— Works of, 8 vols.
—— Sir George S.—Iceland, Travels in, 4to.
—— Mrs. Colin—India, Six Years in, 3 vols.
Mackintosh, Sir J.—England, History of, 10 vols.
———— Miscellaneous Works of
———— Life of, 2 vols.
Macmichael, W.—Moscow to Constantinople, Journey from, 4to.
Macmillan's Magazine, 1868 to 1882.
Macnish, Robert—Sleep, Philosophy of
Macpherson, James—State Papers, 2 vols., 4to.
Macready, W. C., Reminiscences & Diaries of, 2 vols. *Pollock*.
Madagascar, History of, 2 vols. ....*Ellis*.
———— Revisited .... ,,
———— Three Visits to .... ,,
Madan, Martin—Executive Justice, Thoughts on
Madden, R. R.—United Irishmen, Lives and Times of, 7 vols.
———— Turkey, &c., Travels in, 2 vols.
———— Infirmities of Genius, 2 vols
———— Blessington, Countess of, Life, &c., of, 3 vols.
Madoc ....*Southey*.
Madras, Letters from, by a Lady.
Maffei, Count—Brigand Life in Italy, 2 vols.

Man, Observations on, 3 vols. ....*Hartley.*
—— Varieties of, Natural History of ....*Latham.*
—— of Feeling ....*Mackenzie.*
—— Isle of, Account of ....*Woods.*
————— Tour through ....*Feltham.*
Manchester, Country round, Description of, 4to. ......*Aikin.*
————— Literary Society of, Memoirs of, 8 vols.
————— D. of—Court & Society from Eliz. to Anne, 2 vols.
Mandeville, a Tale of the 17th Century, 3 vols. ......*Godwin.*
Manfred ....*Byron.*
Manilla and Japan, A Lady's Visit to ....*Anna D'A.*
Mann, Sir Horace, Letters to, 2 series, 7 vols. ......*Walpole.*
Man's Power over himself to prevent Insanity.
—— Nature & Development, Laws of...*Atkinson & Martineau.*
Mansfield, William Earl of, Life of, 4to. ....*Holliday.*
————— Lord, Letters to, 4to. ....*Stuart.*
————— Park, 3 vols. ....*Austen.*
Mantell, Dr. G. A.—Medals of Creation, 2 vols.
————————— Geology, Wonders of, 2 vols.
Manufacturing Districts, Tour through the, 2 vols. ......*Head.*
Manuscripts in the Harleian Collection, Catalogue of, 4 vols., fo.
Many Thoughts on Many Things, 4to. ....*Southgate.*
Manzoni, A.—The Betrothed Lovers, 2 vols.
————— The Column of Infamy.
Marcet, Mrs. —Land and Water, Conversations on
————— Vegetable Physiology, Conversations on
Marchioness of Brinvilliers ....*A. Smith.*
Marco Polo, Travels of, 4to. ....*Marsden.*
Margaret Catchpole, History of, 2 vols.
————— Graham ....*James.*
————— Ravenscroft ....*St. John.*
Marie Antoinette, Memoirs of, 2 vols. ....*Campan.*
Marienbad, Mineral Waters of ....*Herzig.*
Mariner, Wm.—Tonga Islands, Account of Natives of, 2 vols.

Marino Faliero, the Doge of Venice ....*Byron.*

———————— with Prophecy of Dante .... ,,

Maritime and Inland Discovery, 3 vols.

Mark Wilton, or the Merchant's Clerk ....*Tayler.*

Markham, Mrs.—France, History of

——————— Germany, History of

——————— Col. Fred.—Himalayas, Shooting in the

———————— Albert H.—Whaling Cruise to Baffin's Bay.

———————— C. R.—Cuzco and Lima.

Mark's Reef ....*Cooper.*

Marlborough, Duchess of, Memoirs of, 2 yols. ......*Thomson.*

———————— Duke of, Military Life of ....*Alison.*

———————————— Memoirs of, 6 vols. and Atlas ...*Coxe.*

Marmion, a Poem ....*Scott.*

Marmont, Marshal—Turkish Empire, Present State of, 1834.

Marmontel, J. F., Memoirs of, 4 vols.

Marocco, Account of Empire of, 4to. ....*Jackson.*

Maroons, History of the, 2 vols. ....*Dallas.*

Marquesas Islands, Residence in ....*Melville.*

Marriage, 2 vols. ....*Ferrier.*

——————— in High Life, with Confessions ....*Bury.*

Marryat, Capt.—America, Diary in, 3 vols.

——————— King's Own.

——————— Naval Officer, 3 vols.

——————— Newton Forster.

——————— Rattlin the Reefer, with Three Cutters.

——————— Smith, Sir Sidney, Memoirs of, 2 vols.

——————— Snarleyow, or Dog Fiend.

———— Frank S.—Borneo and Indian Archipelago.

Marsden, Wm.—Marco Polo, Travels of, 4to.

——————— Sumatra, History of, 4to.

Marsh, Rev. William, D.D., Life of

Marshall, Ebenezer—Union of England & Scotland, History of

——————— John—Washington, Life of General, 5 vols.

Marshall, William—Norfolk, Rural Economy of, 2 vols.
———————— Yorkshire, ,, ,, 2 vols.
Marshland, Great Law of, 1714.
Marston, J. E.—Blucher, Marshal, Life and Campaigns of
Martin, Benjamin—Philosophia Britannica, 3 vols.
——— John—Tonga Islands, Account of, 2 vols.
——— R. M.—British Colonies, History of, 5 vols.
——————— Ireland, Before and After the Union.
——— Chuzzlewit, 2 vols. ....*Dickens.*
Martineau, Harriet—Addresses, with Prayers and Hymns.
——————— Deerbrook, 3 vols.
——————— Devotional Exercises.
——————— Five Years of Youth.
——————— Hour and the Man, 3 vols.
——————— Life in the Sick Room.
——————— Retrospect of Western Travel, 3 vols
——— James—Endeavours after the Christian Life.
——————— The Rationale of Religious Enquiry.
Martyn, Rev. H., Memoirs of
——— Thomas—Italy, Tour through
Martyr of Antioch, a Poem ....*Milman.*
Mary Barton, 2 vols. ....*Gaskell.*
——— Campbell, the Affectionate Grand-Daughter.
——— Queen of Scots, Letters of, 3 vols. ....*Strickland.*
——————— Life of, 3 vols. ....*Chalmers.*
——— Stuart, Biographical Sketch of ....*Lamartine.*
Mason, William—Poems, 3 vols.
——————— Whitehead, Wm., Memoirs and Poems of
——————— Works of, 4 vols., 1811.
Masque of Pandora, and other Poems ....*Longfellow.*
Massey, Gerald—Babe Christabel, and other Poems.
Massinger, Sir P.—Plays, 4 vols.
——— and Ford, Dramatic Works of
Masson, David—English Poets, Essays on

Masson, David—Milton, Life of, & History of his Time, vol. i

Master Humphrey's Clock, 2 vols., 1840 ....*Dickens*

Materia Medica, History of, 4to. ....*Hill*

Matthews, Charles (the elder), Life and Correspondence of

———— Henry—Diary of an Invalid.

Matrimony, Twelve Months of ....*Carlen.*

Matter to Spirit, From ....*C. D.*

Maturin, Charles R.—Sermons.

Maud, and other Poems ....*Tennyson.*

Maunder, Samuel—Biographical Treasury.

Maurice, F. D.—Lectures on the Religions of the World.

———————— Modern Philosophy.

———————— On the Epistle to the Hebrews.

———————— Sermon on the Lord's Prayer.

———————— Sermons on the Prayer Book.

———————— Theological Essays.

———————— What is Revelation ?

———————————————————— Sequel to

——— Thomas—Hindostan, History of, vol. i., 4to.

Mauritius and back, Transport Voyage to the, pamphlet.

Maw, Henry L.—Pacific to the Atlantic, Passage from

Mawe, John—Diamonds and Precious Stones, Treatise on

——— Thomas—Gardener's Calendar, or Practical Gardener.

Mawman, J.—Highlands of Scotland, Excursion to

Maximilian in Mexico, With ....*Alvensleben.*

Maxwell, W. H.—Wellington, Life of Duke of, 3 vols.

May, Thomas—Long Parliament, History of, 4to.

——— you like it ....*Taylor.*

Mayhew, Henry—London Labour and London Poor, 2 vols.

Maynard, Walter—The Enterprising Impresario.

Mayo, H.—Popular Superstitions, with Account of Mesmerism.

Mazarine Cardinal, History of ....*Taylor.*

Mazeppa ....*Byron.*

McClintock, F. L.—Voyage of the Fox in search of Franklin.

McClintock, F. L.—Discovery of the Fate of Sir John Franklin.
McCrie, Thomas—Knox, John, Life of, 2 vols.
McCullagh, W. T.—Sheil, Richard L., Later Memoirs of
McCulloch, J. R.—British Empire, Statistical Account of, 2 vols.
McGhee, Rev. R. J. L.—How we got to Pekin in 1860.
McGregor, John—America, British, 2 vols.
McGrigor, Sir J., Autobiography of
McLeod, John—Alceste, Voyage in the
Mead, Richard—Medical Works, 3 vols., 1765.
Meadley, G. W.—Paley, William, D.D., Memoirs of
Mechanics ....*Lardner.*
Medals of Creation, 2 vols. ....*Mantell.*
Medhurst, W. H.—The Foreigner in Far Cathay.
Medical Essays, 2 vols , 1745 ....*Mihles.*
—— Observations and Enquiries, vol. ii.
—— Student, The ....*Smith.*
—— Works, 3 vols., 1765 ....*Mead.*
———— folio, 1678 ....*Parey.*
Medici, Lorenzo de, Life of, 2 vols., 4to. ....*Roscoe.*
———————— Illustrations of Life of .... ,,
—— House of, Memoirs of ....*Noble.*
Medicine, Modern Domestic ....*Graham.*
—— Domestic ....*Buchan.*
Medicines, Touchstone of, 1687 ....*Floyer.*
Medinah and Mecca, Pilgrimage to, 3 vols. ....*Burton.*
Meditations and Contemplations ....*Hervey.*
Mediterranean, Excursions in the, 2 vols. ....*Temple.*
———— Letters from the, 2 vols. ....*Blaquiere.*
———— Travels along the, 2 vols. ....*Richardson.*
———— Voyage along the Shores of, 2 vols. ...*Wilde.*
—————————— up the, 4to. ....*Willyams.*
Medusa Frigate, Account of Loss of
Medwin, Thomas—Byron at Pisa, Conversations of, 2 vols.
Meissner, N. N. W.—Dictionary, German and English.

Melcombe, Lord (George Bubb Doddington), Diary of

Melmoth the Wanderer, 4 vols.

Melville, Herman—Marquesas Islands, Residence in

———————— Omoo, or Adventures in the South Seas.

Memorials of a Quiet Life, 2 vols. ....*Hare.*

Men and Manners in America, 2 vols.

———— Women, 2 vols. ....*R. Browning.*

—— Women, and Books, 2 vols. ....*L. Hunt.*

—— I have known ....*Jerdan.*

—— of Genius, 2 vols. ... .*I. D'Israeli.*

—— of the Time, 5 editions, 1857 to 1868.

—— of Letters, time of George III., 2 vols. ......*Brougham.*

Mental Physiology, Chapters on ....*Holland.*

Mentone, &c., as Winter Climates ....*Bennet.*

Mercier, M.—Paris, New Picture of, 2 vols.

Meredith, Mrs. Chas.—My Home in Tasmania, 2 vols.

——————————— New South Wales, Notes & Sketches of

———— George—Modern Love, and other Poems.

—— Owen—*See*, Lytton, Robert B.

Merryweather, F. S.—Misers, Lives and Anecdotes of

Mesmeric State, Surgical Operations in ....*Elliotson.*

Mesmerism and its Opponents .. ..*Sandby.*

——————— in India ....*Esdaile.*

————— in its relation to Health and Disease ...*Neilson.*

——————— Curative Powers of ....*Capern.*

——————— Facts in ....*Townshend.*

——————— Proved True .... ,,

Mesopotamia, Travels in, 4to. ....*Buckingham.*

Messiah, a Poem ....*Montgomery.*

Metal, Manufactures in, 3 vols.

Metcalfe, Chas., Lord, Life & Correspondence of, 2 vols. *Kaye.*

———— Rev. F.—Oxonian in Thelemarken, 2 vols.

——————————————— Norway, 2 vols.

Meteorological Circular, Fenland, 1874—1877, 2 vols. *Miller.*

Meteorology & Causes of Mortality at Wisbech, 13 vols. *Miller*.

Methodism, Portraiture of ....*Nightingale*.

Meunier, V.—Great Hunting Grounds of the World.

Mexico, Conquest of, 3 vols. ....*Prescott*.

—— Court of ....*Kollonitz*.

—— in 1827, 2 vols. ....*Ward*.

—— Interior of, Travels in ....*Hardy*.

—— Life in ....*De La Barca*.

—— Six Months' Residence in ....*Bullock*.

—— and the Rocky Mountains, Adventures in ...*Ruxton*.

Miall, Edward—Editor Off the Line, or Wayside Musings.

———— Bases of Belief.

Michael Angelo considered as a Philosophical Poet.

Michaux, F. A.—America, Travels in West of

Michelet, M.—France, History of, 2 vols.

———— Martin Luther, Life of

Middle Ages, Literary History of, 4to. ....*Berington*.

———— State of Europe during the, 3 vols. ....*Hallam*.

———— ———— ———— Supplemental Notes to ,,

Middlemarch ....*Eliot*.

Middleton, Conyers—Cicero, Life of, 2 vols.

———— and Melmoth—Cicero, Life and Letters of

Midwifery, Theory and Practice of, 1752 ....*Smellie*.

———— Plates to illustrate, folio, 1754 .... ,,

Mignan, Capt. Robert—Chaldea, Travels in

Mihles, S.—Medical Essays, 2 vols., 1745.

Miles, W. A.—Prince of Wales, Letter to, 1808.

Milesian Chief, The, 4 vols.

Milford Haven, Tour to ....*Morgan*.

Military Adventure, Twelve Years of, 2 vols.

—— Commanders, British, 3 vols. ....*Gleig*.

—— Life, Events of a, 2 vols. ....*Henry*.

—— Mentor, 2 vols.

—— Policy of the British Empire ....*Pasley*.

Millar, John—Ranks, Origin of, with Life of Author.
Miller, Joseph—Botanicum Officinale (Herbal.)
—— Thomas—Beauties of the Country.
—— Mrs. M.—Italy, Letters from, 2 vols.
—— General, Memoirs of, 2 vols.
—— Hugh—Footprints of the Creator.
———— My Schools and Schoolmasters.
———— Testimony of the Rocks.
—— S. H.—Evaporation, Prize Essay on
———— Meteorological Observations, 1861-73, 13 vols.
———— Fenland Meteorological Circular, 1874-7, 2 vols.
———— and Skertchly—Fenland, Past and Present.
Millers, George—Ely, Cathedral Church of
Mills, Charles—Muhammedanism, History of
Milman, Dean—Anne Boleyn, a Poem.
———— Belshazzar, a Dramatic Poem.
———— Christianity, History of, 3 vols.
———— ———— Latin, History of, 6 vols.
———— Fazio, with the Fall of Jerusalem.
———— Jerusalem, Fall of
———— Jews, History of the, 3 vols.
———— Martyr of Antioch.
———— Samor, Lord of the Bright City.
———— Poetical Works of
Milner, Dean, Life of
—— Rev. Joseph—Church of Christ, History of, 4 vols.
Milnes, R. M. (Lord Houghton)—Poetry for the People, &c.
———— Keats, John, Life and Remains of, 2 vols.
Milton, John—Christian Doctrine, Treatise on, 4to.
———— Paradise Lost.
———— Poetical Works, 6 vols.
———— Smaller Poems.
———— Prose Works, 1697, folio.
———— Works of, 8 vols., 1759.

Mitchell, Lieut.-Col. J.—Wallenstein, A., Life of
——— Major T. L.—Australia, E., 3 Expeditions to, 2 vols.
——— and Dickie—Witchcraft, Philosophy of
Mitford, William—Greece, History of, 3 vols., 4to.
——— Mary R.—Our Village, 2 vols. in 1.
——————— Literary Life, Recollections of, 2 vols.
——————— Life of, 3 vols.
——————— Rienzi, pamphlet.
——— A. B.—Old Japan, Tales of, 2 vols.
——— Rev. J.—Gray, T., and Mason, W., Correspondence of
Moab, Land of ....*Tristram.*
Modern Griselda ....*Edgeworth.*
——— Love, and other Poems ....*Meredith.*
Moens, W.J.C.—English Travellers & Italian Brigands, 2 vols.
Moffat, Robert—Africa, Missionary Labours in Southern
Mogul Empire, Travels in the, 2 vols. ....*Bernier.*
Moleville, A. F. B. de—Louis XVI., Last Years of, 3 vols.
Monachism, British, 4to. ....*Fosbrooke.*
Monarchs Retired from Business, 2 vols. ....*Doran.*
Monarchy of the Middle Classes (France), 2 vols. *H.L.Bulwer.*
Monasteries in the Levant, Visit to ....*Curzon.*
Monastery, The, 3 vols. ....*Scott.*
Monastic Life, Economy of, 4to. ....*Fosbrooke.*
Monk, The, 3 vols. ....*Lewis.*
——— James H.—Bentley, Richard, D.D., Life of, 4to.
Monke, G. P.—Voltaire, M. de, Life of
Monkeys, Anecdotes of
Monks and Giants ....*W. and R. Whistlecroft.*
Monographs, Personal and Social ....*Houghton.*
Monro, Rev. Vere—Syria, Summer Ramble in, 2 vols.
——— Alex.—Anatomy of the Bones and Nerves, 2 vols.,1758.
Mont Blanc, Ascent of ....*Hudson and Kennedy.*
——————— Story of ....*A. Smith.*
Montagu, George—Ornithological Dictionary, 3 vols.

Montagu, Mrs. Elizabeth, Letters of
Montague, Lady Mary W., Letters of, 1779.
———————————————————— and Works of, 1767.
Montesquieu, M. de—Persian Letters, 2 vols.
———————— On the Spirit of the Laws, 2 vols.
Montgomery, James—Original Hymns.
———————————— Poems of, 4 vols.
———————————— World before the Flood, a Poem.
———————————— Poetry, &c., Lectures on
———————————— Prose by a Poet, 2 vols.
———————————— Gleanings from Pious Authors.
————————— Robert—God and Man.
———————————— Gospel in Advance of the Age.
———————————— Messiah, a Poem.
———————————— Omnipresence of the Deity.
———————————— Selections from Poetical Works of
Montholon, Count—Napoleon at St. Helena, 4 vols.
Monumental Brasses and Slabs ....*Boutell*.
Moodie, Susannah—Roughing it in the Bush, 2 vols.
Moorcroft, Wm.—Bokhara and Hindostan, Travels in, 2 vols.
Moore, James—Campaign of the British Army in Spain.
——— John—Journal when in France, 2 vols.
——————— France & Italy, Society & Manners in, 4 vols.
——————— French Revolution, Causes & Progress, 2 vols.
——— Sir John, Life of, 2 vols.
——— Thomas—Anacreon, Odes of, 2 vols.
——————— Byron, Lord, Life and Letters of, 2 vols., 4to.
——————— Epicurean, a Tale.
——————— Fitzgerald, Lord Edward, Life of, 2 vols.
——————— Ireland, History of, 4 vols.
——————— Loves of the Angels.
——————— Memoirs, Journal & Correspondence, 8 vols.
——————— Poetical Works, 1 vol.
—————————————— 10 vols.

Moore, Thomas—Sheridan, R. B., Life of, 2 vols.
———————— Zeluco; Views of Human Nature, 2 vols.
Moorland Cottage, The
Moral Evil, Enquiry into Causes of
—— Tales, 2 vols. ....*Edgeworth.*
More, Hannah—Cœlebs in Search of a Wife, 2 vols.
———————— Christian Morals.
———————— Sacred Dramas.
———————— Memoirs of, 4 vols. ....*Roberts.*
—— Sir T.—Utopia, 1751.
—— Worlds than One ....*Brewster.*
Morell, Sir Charles—*See,* Ridley, Rev. James.
—— Thomas—Philosophy and Science, History of
Morgan, A. de—Probabilities, Essay on
—— Mrs. Mary—Milford Haven, Tour to
—— Lady—Absenteeism.
———————— Florence Macarthy, 4 vols.
———————— France, 2 vols.
———————— Italy, Journal of a Residence in, 3 vols.
———————— O'Donnell, 3 vols.
———————— Salvator Rosa, Life and Times of, 2 vols.
———————— The Missionary, an Indian Tale, 3 vols.
———————— Wild Irish Girl.
———————— Memoirs of, 2 vols.
—— Sidney, Autobiography of
Morier, J.—Abel Allnutt, 3 vols.
Mormons, or Latter Day Saints.
Mornings in Spring, 2 vols. ....*Drake.*
Morocco, Travels in, and Residence in the Esmailla ...*Scott.*
Morris, E. Joy—Turkey and Greece, Tour through
—— Rev. F. O.—Nests and Eggs of British Birds, 3 vols.
—— William—Earthly Paradise, 4 vols.
Morsels of Criticism on New Testament, 2 vols., 4to., 1788. *King.*
Morus; Disputations on Christian Chivalry, 1826 ......*Digby.*

187

Moscheles, I.—Beethoven, Life of, 2 vols.
Moscow to Constantinople, Journey from ....*Macmichael.*
Moses as an Historian, Character of ....*J. Townshend.*
Mosses and Corals, General History of, 4to., 1768 ...*Dillenius.*
———— from an Old Manse ....*Hawthorne.*
Motions of Animals, Essay on ....*Whytt.*
Motley, John L.—Dutch Republic, Rise of the, 3 vols.
———————— United Netherlands, History of, 4 vols.
Moultrie, John—Altars, Hearths, and Homes.
———————— Dream of Life, and other Poems.
Mount of Olives ....*Hamilton.*
Mountain Bard, The ....*Hogg.*
Mouse, Life and Perambulations of a
Mozart, W. A., Letters of
———— and Haydn, Lives of
Mr. Ledbury, Adventures of ....*Smith.*
Mrs. Armitage, or Female Domination ....*Mrs. Gore.*
———— Halliburton's Troubles ....*Mrs. H. Wood.*
———— Leicester's School.
———— Matthews ....*Mrs. Trollope.*
Mudie, James—Felony of New South Wales.
———— Robert—British Naturalist, 2 vols.
Muhammedanism, History of ....*Mills.*
Muller, Max—Chips from a German Workshop, 2 vols.
———————— Science of Language, Lectures on, 2 vols.
Muloch, Miss (Mrs. Craik)—Life for a Life, 3 vols.
———————————— Lord Erlistoun, &c.
———————————— The Ogilvies.
Mundy, G. C.—Our Antipodes, or Rambles in Australia, 3 vols.
Munich, Social Life in ....*E. Wilberforce.*
Munro, Sir Thomas, Life of, 3 vols. ....*Gleig.*
Murat, Joachim, Fall and Death of ....*Macirone.*
Murchison, Sir R.—Siluria.
Murphy, Arthur—Garrick, David, Life of, 2 vols.

Murphy, Arthur—Johnson, Dr. Samuel, Life and Genius of
———————— Works of, 7 vols.
Murray, Alexander—Bruce, James, Life of, 4to.
——— Hon. Charles A.—America, Travels in North, 2 vols.
——— Hugh—Africa, Discoveries and Travels in, 2 vols.
——————— Asia, Discoveries in, 3 vols.
——————— Geography, Encyclopædia of
——— James E.—Pyrenees, Summer in the, 2 vols.
——— John—Eastern Counties, Handbook of, 1870.
——————— Europe, Northern, Handbook of, 3 vols., 1849.
——————— France, Handbook of, 1858.
——————— Germany, Northern, Handbook of, 1865.
————————— Southern,   ,,   ,, 1851.
——————— Italy, Central, and Rome, Handbook of, 1850.
——————— Sardinia, Lombardy, Venice,   ,,   1856.
——————— Tuscany and Florence, Handbook of, 1856.
——— Hon. Mrs. M.—Scotland, Guide to Beauties of, 2 vols.
——— Pattrick J.—Banim, John, Life of
——— Lindley, Memoirs of
——— Robert D.—Port Philip, Summer at
Muscologia Britannica; Mosses of Britain. *Hooker & Taylor.*
Musgrave, Sir R.—Ireland, Rebellions in, 4to.
Music, History of
——— General History of, 4 vols., 4to. ....*Burney.*
——— Popular, of the Olden Times, 2 vols., 4to. ...*Chappell.*
——— and Morals ....*Haweis.*
——— and Manners in France & Germany, 3 vols. ...*Chorley.*
Musical History, Biography, and Criticism ....*Hogarth.*
——— Recollections, Thirty Years', 2 vols. ....*Chorley.*
——— and Personal Recollections, 2 vols. ....*Phillips.*
Musæus, J. C. A.—Libussa, and other Tales.
Mussulmauns of India, Observations on, 2 vols. ...*Hassen Ali.*
Musters, George C.—Patagonians, At Home with the
My Novel, 4 vols. ....*Lytton.*

Myographia, or a Description of the Muscles, about 1740.
Mysoor, History of, 3 vols., 4to. ....*Wilks.*
Mysteries of Udolpho, 4 vols. ....*Radcliffe.*
Mysterious Mother, a Tragedy.
Mystery, The ....*Young.*
Mystic, The, and other Poems ....*Bailey.*

NALSON, J.—Charles I., Trial of, 1740.
Napier, Sir C. J.—Ionian Islands, On the
————————— Scinde, Conquest of
——— Col. Eliers—Africa, Excursions in South, 2 vols.
——— W. F. P.—Peninsular War, History of, 6 vols.
Naples, Tour through, 4to. ....*Craven.*
Napoleon I.—*See,* Bonaparte.
——— III.—Julius Cæsar, History of, 2 vols.
Nares, Rev. E.—Burghley, Lord, (Wm. Cecil), Life, &c., 3 vols.
Nathalie, 3 vols. ....*Kavanagh.*
National Defence, System of, 2 vols. ....*Macdiarmid.*
——— Improvement, Plan of, 4to.
——— Tales, 2 vols. ....*Hood.*
Natural History, On the Study of, 2 vols. ....*Swainson.*
——————— Essays on, 2 vols. ....*Waterton.*
——————— Dissertations on, 2 vols. ....*Spallanzani.*
——————— Philosophy of, 2 vols., 4to. ....*Smellie.*
——————— Tracts relative to, 4to., 1793 ......*Falconer.*
——————— Magazine of, 3 vols.
——————— Gleanings in, 2 vols. ....*Jesse.*
——————— Contributions to, by a Rural D.D.
——————— Curiosities of, 3 series, 4 vols. ...*Buckland.*
——————— of Animals & Vegetables, 2 vols. *Spallanzani.*
——————— of Selborne, 2 vols. ....*White.*
——————— and Geology, Researches into ......*Darwin.*
——— Philosophy, Introduction to, 2 vols. ....*Nicholson.*
——————— Discourse on the Study of ...*Herschell.*

Nepaul, Kingdom of, History of, 4to. ....*Kirkpatrick.*
Nests and Eggs of British Birds, 3 vols. ....*Morris.*
Netherlands, Gazetteer of the, 1794.
———— History of the ....*Grattan.*
————————————— United, 4 vols. ....*Motley.*
New Cratylus, The ....*Donaldson.*
—— England, &c., Travels in, 4 vols. ....*Dwight.*
—— Monthly Magazine, 1819—1823, 12 vols.
————————— 1841, 1842, 2 vols.
—— South Wales, Description of ....*Wentworth.*
——————————— Gazetteer of ....*Whitworth.*
——————————— Memoirs on ....*Field.*
——————————— Notes and Sketches of ....*Meredith.*
——————————— Rambles and Observations in ...*Townsend.*
——————————— Two Years' Residence in, 2 vols. *Cunningham.*
——————————— Wanderings in, 2 vols. ....*Bennett.*
——————————— Department of Mines, Report of, 1877-79.
—— Spain, Political Essay on, 4 vols. ....*Humboldt.*
—— York, Knickerbocker's History of, 2 vols. ....*Irving.*
—— Zealand, Adventure in, 2 vols. ....*Wakefield.*
——————— British Colonization of
——————— and its Inhabitants ....*Taylor.*
——————— the Britain of the South, 2 vols. ...*Hursthouse.*
——————— Travels in, 2 vols. ....*Dieffenbach.*
——————— and Adventures in, 2 vols. ...*Polack.*
Newby, Mrs.—Common Sense.
Newcomes, The, 2 vols. ....*Thackeray.*
Newfoundland, History of ....*Anspach.*
——————— in 1842, 2 vols. ....*Bonnycastle.*
Newgate Calendar, 5 vols. ....*Knapp and Baldwin.*
——————————— The New, 1863—1865.
Newman, F. W.—Phases of Truth.
——————— The Soul, her Sorrows and her Aspirations.
——————— Fredk.—England, Curiosities and Beauties of, folio.

Nile, Travels to discover Source of, Plates to illustrate. *Bruce.*

——Discovery of Source of ....*Speke.*

Nina, 2 vols. ....*Bremer.*

Nineteenth Century, 1880—1882.

Nineveh and Babylon, Discoveries in ....*Layard.*

—— and its Remains, 2 vols. .... ,,

—— and Persepolis ....*Vaux.*

—— &c., Two Years' Residence at, 2 vols. ......*Fletcher.*

No Name, 3 vols. ....*Collins.*

Noble, Mark—Cromwell, Memoirs of House of, 2 vols.

———— Medici, Memoirs of House of

——Families, Vicissitudes of, 3 vols. ....*Burke.*

Nodier, Charles—Bean Flower and Pea Blossom.

Nollekens and his Times, 2 vols. ....*Smith.*

Noontide Leisure, 2 vols. ....*Drake.*

Norfolk Charities, Account of ....*Clark.*

—— County Rate, Statistical Tables of ....*Kitton.*

—— Rural Economy of, 2 vols. ....*Marshall.*

—— Topographical History of, 11 vols. ....*Blomefield.*

Norris, Amelia—The Early Start in Life.

—— Maria—Madame de Stael, Life and Times of

North, Christopher—*See,* Wilson, John.

———————— Recreations of, 3 vols. ....*Wilson.*

———————— Memoirs of, 2 vols. ....*Mrs. Gordon.*

——Pole, Voyage towards ....*Phipps.*

——West Passage by Land ....*Milton and Cheadle.*

———————— Voyage in Search of, 4to. ....*Parry.*

———————— Journal of Parry's First Voyage. *Fisher.*

———————— Second Voyage, 4to. ....*Parry.*

———————— Third Voyage, 4to. .... ,,

———————— Mc Clure's Discovery of ....*Osborn.*

———————— Discovery of, Narrative of ...*Armstrong.*

———————— and Search for Franklin ....*Brown.*

Northanger Abbey, with Persuasion, 4 vols. ....*Austen.*

Norths, Lives of the, under Charles II. and James II., 3 vols.

Norton, Hon. Mrs.—Dream, and other Poems.

———————— Child of the Islands.

——————— Lady of La Garaye.

——————— Stuart of Dunleath.

—————— Andrews—Genuineness of the Gospels, Evidences of

Norway and its Glaciers visited in 1851 ....*Forbes.*

—————— Kings of, Chronicles of, 3 vols. ....*Laing.*

—————— Sweden, &c., Letters on ....*Wollstonecraft.*

—————— Residence in ....*Laing.*

—————— Unprotected Females in

Not so bad as we seem, a Comedy ....*Lytton.*

Notes and Queries, 1849—1855; 1868, 1869, 16 vols.

——— of a Traveller in Prussia, France, &c. ....*Laing.*

——— of a Wanderer in Search of Health, 2 vols. ...*Cumming.*

——— during a Ramble in Germany.

Nott, Sir William, Memoirs of, 2 vols. ....*Stocqueler.*

Novels and Novelists from Eliz. to Victoria, 2 vols. *Jeaffreson.*

——————— Tales ....*Goëthe.*

Novum Organum, with Advancement of Learning ......*Bacon.*

Now and Then ....*Warren.*

Nubia, Travels in ....*Burckhardt.*

Nubian Dessert, Ride through ....*Peel.*

Numismatic Chronicle, 9 vols. in 3 ....*Akerman.*

———————————— July, 1847 ....   ,,

Nursery Rhymes with Tunes, edited by Rimbault.

Nutt, Thomas—Bees, The Management of

OATES, Titus, & others—Narratives of the Popish Plot, 1629.

Oaths, Origin and History of ....*Tyler.*

Oberon, from the German of Wieland, 2 vols.

Observer, The, 5 vols., 1786—1790.

Occult Philosophy, Three Books of, 1651 ......*H. C. Agrippa.*

—————————— Fourth Book of, 1783 ......   ,,

Oceola Nikkanochee, Narrative of
Ocean, Atmosphere, and Life, 2 vols. ....*Reclus.*
Odd Journeys ....*Hollingshead.*
——People ....*Reid.*
Ode to Bonaparte ....*Byron.*
Odes, Probationary, for the Laureateship ....*Hawkins.*
O'Donnell, 3 vols. ....*Morgan.*
O'Driscol, John—Ireland, Views of, 2 vols.
Ogilvies, The ....*Muloch.*
Ogle, Nathaniel—Christ's Sermon on the Mount.
Old Curiosity Shop, 2 vols. ....*Dickens.*
— English Baron, &c. ....*Reeve.*
— Leaves gathered from Household Words ....*Wills.*
— Maids, Essays on, 3 vols.
— Mortality ....*Scott.*
— Testament, Essay on, 1722 ....*Whiston.*
———————— Characters, Legends of, 2 vols. *Baring-Gould.*
— and New Testament, Authentic Records on, 2 vols., 1727.
Oliphant, Lawrence—Russian Shores of Black Sea.
———————— Mrs.—Irving, Rev. Edward, Life of
Oliver Newman ....*Southey.*
— Old School, Portfolio of, 1801-2, 4to.
— Twist ....*Dickens.*
Ollivant, J. E.—Breeze from the Great Salt Lake.
O'Meara, Barry E.—Napoleon in Exile, 2 vols.
———————————————— Historical Memoirs of, 1815.
Omniana, 2 vols. ....*Southey.*
Omnipresence of the Deity ....*R. Montgomery.*
Omoo, or Adventures in the South Seas ....*Melville.*
One in a Thousand ....*James.*
Opie, Amelia—Lays for the Dead.
———————— Poems.
———————— Warrior's Return, and other Poems.
———————— Life of ....*Brightwell.*

Ovid's Metamorphoses, 2 vols., translated by Howard.

———————————— First Two Books, translated by Mills.

Owen, R. Dale—Footfalls on the Boundary of another World.

Owhyhee, *see* Hawaii.

Oxford, Memorials of, 3 vols. ....*Ingram.*

Oxonian in Norway, 2 vols. ....*Metcalfe.*

——— in Thelemarken, 2 vols. .... „

Oxoniana, 4 vols.

Oyster, The, Where to Find, Breed, and Cook it.

PACIFIC to the Atlantic, Passage from ....*Maw.*

——— Voyage to the, 2 vols. ....*Beechey.*

Page, David—Geology, Introductory Text Book of

———————— ——— Advanced Text Book of

——————— Geological Terms, Handbook of

—— Thomas—Improvement of River Nene, Report on

Paget, John—Hungary and Transylvania, 2 vols.

Paine, Thomas—Letter to the Abbé Raynal.

Painted Window, a Poem ....*Arnold.*

Painters, Century of, 2 vols. ....*R. and S. Redgrave.*

——— Our Living

——— Dictionary of, 4to. ....*Pilkington.*

——— and Engravers, Dictionary of ....*Bryan.*

Painting, An Idea of the Perfection of ....*J. Evelyn.*

——— and the Fine Arts ....*Haydon and Hazlitt.*

——— in Italy, History of, 6 vols. ....*Lanzi.*

——— Lectures on, 4to. ....*Fuseli.*

———————— by Barry, Opie, and Fuseli.

Palestine, or the Holy Land ....*Russell.*

——— and Lebanon, Three Weeks in

——— Exiles of, 3 vols.

Paley, William—Christianity, Evidences of, 2 vols.

——————— Natural Theology.

————————— ——————— illustrated, 2 vols.

Paley, William—Philosophy, Moral and Political, 4to.

————————— Works of, 6 vols.

————————— Memoirs of ....*Meadley.*

Palgrave, W. G.—Arabia, Travels in Central & Eastern, 2 vols.

————— Fras.—Writs, Parliamentary & Military, 3 vols., fo.

Pallas, Dr.—Russian Sheep, Account of

Palmer, E. H.—Desert of the Exodus, 2 vols.

Palmerston, Viscount, Life of, 2 vols. ....*H. L. Bulwer.*

Paltock, Robert—Wilkins, Peter, Life and Adventures of

Pamela, 4 vols. ....*Richardson.*

Pamphlets, Miscellaneous, containing :—

    The Baviad, by Gifford.

    Thoughts on the Manners of the Great.

    Account of Stratford-upon-Avon.

Pamphlets, Miscellaneous, 4to., containing :—

    Bigland's Observations on Marriages, Baptisms, and Burials.

    List of Contributors to the Defence of the Country in 1588.

    Seetzen's Account of the Lake of Tiberias, &c.

    Wardrop's Account of James Mitchell.

Pamphlets, Miscellaneous, 14 vols., containing :—

  1.—Howlett's Inquiry respecting Inclosures.

      Gillingwater on Parish Workhouses.

      Tooke's Two Pair of Portraits.

      Prospects on the Rubicon.

      Lofft's Letters on the Regency.

      Royal Recollections.

  2.—Lofft's Remarks on Burke's Reflections.

      Letters of Brutus.

      Miller's (Sir J. Rigg's) Speeches on Weights.

      Miller (Sir J. Rigg), Bishop of Auton's Letter to

      Broome on the Impeachment of Warren Hastings.

  3.—Anecdotes of Hume and Lord Chesterfield.

      Man of the World.

      Tooke's Two Pair of Portraits.

Dissertation on Anecdotes.
Trial of the Bishop of Bangor.
Kirwan on Manures.
4.—Letter to Lord Sheffield.
Herculaneum, Description of
——————— Discoveries in, by Venuti.
——————— Destruction of
Farmer's Essay on the Learning of Shakespeare.
5.—Montgaillard on the War.
Letter to the Prince of Wales.
Burke's Letter to a Noble Lord.
Erskine on the War.
York's Letter to the Reformers.
Mirror for Princes.
6.—Nasmith's Charge to the Grand Jury, &c.
Bowles' Reflections.
Canonization of Thomas ——, Esq.
Beddoe's First Essay on Health.
Address to the Deists.
7.—Burges on Catholic Emancipation.
Maltby's Letter to the Freeholders.
Romilly on the Criminal Law.
Observations addressed to Grand Juries.
Roscoe's Considerations.
Randolph's Considerations.
Observations on the Inclosure Act.
8.—Colquhoun on Education.
Vaughan's Siege of Zaragoza.
Commerce and Navigation of the Black Sea.
Dewe's Sermon, "The Sudden Change."
Retreat of the French Army out of Russia.
Dibdin's Bibliomania.
Practical Norfolk Farmer.
Waring's Remarks on Buchanan.

Retrospect of Philosophical Discoveries, No. 1.
Hogan's Appeal.
Refutation of Hogan's Appeal.
9.—Letter to T. W. Coke, Esq., by a Clergyman.
Glover's Answer to ditto.
Burges' Reflections on the Spirit of the Times.
Review of ditto by a Norfolk Freeholder.
Burges' Cato to Lord Byron.
Letter from the King to his People.
Reply to ditto.
Second Letter from the King to his People.
Declaration of the People to the King.
10.—Second Report of the Police Committee.
Report of the Committee on the Poor Laws.
Mainwaring on the Police of the Metropolis.
11.—Mackinnon's Journal of the Campaign in Spain, &c.
Eustace's Letter from Paris.
Some Documents on the late Events in Spain.
Browne's Remarks on the Eclectic Review.
Rennell's Remarks on Scepticism.
12.—Sabine's Remarks on Ross's Voyage.
Buxton's Speech on Punishments.
The State of the Nation in 1822.
Adair's Two Letters to the Bishop of Winchester.
Reply to ditto.
13.—Narrative of the Battle of Leipsic.
Chateaubriand on Bonaparte and the Bourbons.
Bowerbank's Journal on Board the Bellerophon.
Account of the Battle of Waterloo.
Goldsmith's Address to the Sovereigns of Europe.
Liberty, Civil and Religious, by a Friend to both.
14.—Chatfield's Appeal in the Cause of the Greeks.
Malthus on the Corn Laws.
Rose on Banks for Savings.

Park, Mungo—Africa, Mission to, in 1805, 4to.

Parkins, Mansfield—Abyssinia, Life in, 2 vols.

Parley, Peter,(S.G.Goodrich)—Universal History.

————————————————— Tales about Sun,Moon,& Stars.

Parliament of England, 1640, History of, 4to. ....*May.*

—————Key to both Houses of

Parliamentary Portraits.

————————— Writs of Scotland, 1424—1707, 10 vols., folio.

————————— and Military Writs, 3 vols., folio ...*Palgrave.*

Parnell, Dr. Thomas—Poems, with Life by Goldsmith.

Parr, Dr. Saml.—Aphorisms, Opinions, and Reflections.

————————— Bellendenus, Preface to, translated by Beloe.

————————— Memoirs of, 2 vols. ....*Field.*

—————————— Catalogue of Library of

Parry,Rev.R.—Scipio Africanus & Epaminondas,Lives of,2vols.

———— Sir W. E.—North-west Passage, Voyage in Search of,4to.

———————————————————— Second Voyage, 4to.

————————————————————— Third Voyage, 4to.

————————— Voyage in 1827, 4to.

——————————————— Journal of ....*Fisher.*

————————— Memoirs of

———— William—Byron, Lord, The Last Days of

Parson's Daughter, 3 vols. ....*Hook.*

Partington, Charles F.—Steam Engine, On the

Pascal, Blaise—Provincial Letters.

Pasley, C. W.—Military Policy of the British Empire.

Past and Present ....*Carlyle.*

Passions, Treatise on, 2 vols. ....*Cogan.*

Patagonians, At Home with the ....*Musters.*

Patchwork, 3 vols. ....*Hall.*

Patronage, 4 vols. ....*Edgeworth.*

Patrick, Simon—Advice to a Friend, 1677.

Pau, Curative influence of the Climate of ....*Taylor.*

Paul Bedford, Recollections and Wanderings of

Pinkerton, J.—Voyages & Travels, Collection of, 17 vols., 4to.

Pinkney, Lieut.-Col.—France, Travels through, 4to.

Piozzi, Mrs. H. L., Autobiography of, 2 vols.

———— ———— Letters to and from Dr. S. Johnson.

——— ——— ———— France, &c., On a Journey through, 2 vols.

———— ———— Retrospection, 2 vols., 4to.

Piozziana, or Recollections of Mrs. Piozzi.

Pirate ....*Scott.*

Pitcairn's Island, Voyage to ....*Shillibeer.*

Pitt, Wm. (Earl of Chatham), History of, 2 vols., 4to. *Thackeray.*

———— ————————————— Anecdotes of Life of, 4 vols.

———— ———————————— Letters of

————Rt. Hon. Wm., Life of, vols. i. and ii., 4to. ......*Tomline.*

———— ———— Speeches of, in House of Commons, 3 vols.

Plague in London, 1665, History of ....*De Foe.*

Planter's Kalendar ....,...............................*Nicol.*

Plants, Encyclopædia of ....*Loudon.*

Plato, Works of, 5 vols., 4to.

Platts, Rev. J.—Biography, New Universal, 5 vols.

Playfair, Wm.—Atlas, Commercial & Political, fcap. 4to., 1786.

———————— Decline and Fall of Nations, Inquiry into, 4to.

—————— Political Portraits, 3 vols.

Plays, Old English, 6 vols.

Pleasures of Hope ....*Campbell.*

———— Human Life, 1807 ....*Hilaris Benevolus.*

———— Imagination ....*Akenside.*

———— Memory ....*Rogers.*

Pliny, Letters of, 2 vols., translated by Melmoth.

Plot in Private Life, and other Tales ....*Collins.*

Plowden, Francis—Ireland, History of, 3 vols., 4to.

Plumptre, Anne—France, Three Years' Residence in, 3 vols.

Plutarch, Revolutionary, 3 vols.

Plutarch's Lives, 6 vols., translated by Langhorne.

Pocket Book, My, 1808.

Porcelain and Glass.

Porden, Eleanor A.—Cœur de Lion, a Poem, 2 vols.

Port Philip, Summer at ....*Murray.*

Porter, G. R.—Progress of the Nation, 3 vols.

—— Jane—Sir Edward Seaward's Narrative, 3 vols.

—— Sir Robert Ker—Campaign in Russia, 4to.

———————————— Persia, Travels in, 2 vols., 4to.

—— Rev. J. L.—Giant Cities of Bashan.

———————— Damascus, Five Years in

Porteus, Dr. B., Life and Works of, 6 vols.

——————— Bishop of London, Life of

Portfolio of Oliver Old School, 1801, 1802, 4to.

Portugal in 1828 ....*Young.*

—— Defence of ....*Eliot.*

—— Travels in ....*Latouche.*

—— and Galicia, Social and Political ....*Carnarvon.*

Positive Philosophy, translated by H. Martineau ......*Comte.*

Postans, T.—Sindh, Observations on

Pott, Percivall, Chirurgical Works of, 4 vols., 1771.

Potter, John—Greece, Antiquities of, 2 vols.

Poultry, Ornamental and Domestic ....*Dixon.*

Powell, Rev. Baden—Physical Sciences.

——————— Connection of Natural and Divine Truth.

Power, Marguerite—Virginia's Hand, a Poem.

Praed, Winthrop Mackworth, Poems of, 2 vols.

Prairie, The ....*Cooper.*

Pratt, S. J.—Wales, Holland, &c., Gleanings through, 6 vols.

Prayers, selected by Rev. T. Clapham ....*Jer. Taylor.*

Pre-Adamite Earth ....*Harris.*

—————— Man.

Precious Metals, On the, 2 vols. ....*Jacob.*

Prelude, The ....*Wordsworth.*

Prescott, William—Essays, Critical and Historical

——————— Ferdinand and Isabella, History of, 3 vols.

Pyramids of Gizeh, Operations at the, 3 vols. ....*Vyse.*
Pyrenees, The, with Excursions into Spain, 2 vols. *Chatterton.*
————— Letters from the ....*Paris.*
————— Romance of the, 4 vols.
—————— Sketches in, 2 vols.
————— Summer in the, 2 vols. ....*Murray.*
————— ————— and Winter in ....*Ellis.*

Q. Q., Contributions of, 2 vols. ....*Taylor.*
Quadrupeds, History of ....*Bewick.*
————— Natural History & Classification of ...*Swainson.*
Quakerism, or the Story of My Life ....*Mrs. Greer.*
————— Portraiture of, 3 vols. ....*Clarkson.*
Quarterly Review, 1809 to 1882.
Quedah ....*Osborn.*
Queechy ....*Wetherell.*
Queen Mary, a Poem ....*Tennyson.*
Queens of England, 2 vols. ....*Lawrance.*
————————— 12 vols. ....*Strickland.*
————— of Scotland, & Eng. Princesses, 8 vols. (vol. v. missing).
Quentin Durward ....*Scott.*
Quin, M. J.—Steam Voyage down the Danube, 2 vols.
————————— on the Seine, Moselle, &c., 2 vols.
Quincey, Thos. de—Confessions of an English Opium Eater.
————————— Autobiographic Sketches, 2 vols.
Quincy, J.—Dispensatory, English, 1726.
————————— of Royal Coll. of Physicians, 1727.
Quits, by the Author of Initials ....*Tautphœus.*
Quotations, Familiar, Book of

RABELAIS, François, Works of, 2 vols.
Rachel, Madame, (Tragedian), Memoirs of, 2 vols. ...*Barrera.*
Radcliff, Rev. Thomas—Agriculture of Flanders, Report on
Radcliffe, Ann—Castles of Athlin and Dunbayne.

Radcliffe, Ann—Gaston de Blondeville, 4 vols.
———— Mysteries of Udolpho, 4 vols.
———— The Italian, 3 vols.
———— Romance of the Forest, 3 vols.
———— A Sicilian Romance, 2 vols.
———— J. T.—Fiends, Ghosts, and Sprites.
Rae, John—Arctic Expedition in 1846 and 1847.
—— Edward—Land of the North Wind.
Raffles, Sir Stamford—Java, History of, 2 vols., 4to.
———— Life and Services of, by his Widow, 4to.
Ragamuffin, True History of a Little
Raikes, Thos., Diary of, from 1831 to 1847, 4 vols.
———— St. Petersburg, Visit to
———— with Wellington, &c., Private Correspondence of
Raleigh, Sir Walter—Works of, 8 vols.
———— Memoirs of ....*Thomson.*
Rambler, 4 vols., 1793 ....*Johnson.*
Ramsay, Allan—Poems of, 2 vols., 1803.
———— Songs, Scotch and English
—— Rev. James—African Slavery, Essay on
Random Recollections of the House of Commons.
———— Lords.
Ranke, L. von—Popes of Rome, History of, 3 vols.
———— Prussia, History of, 3 vols.
Ranks, Origin of the Distinction of ....*Millar.*
Rape of the Lock ....*Pope.*
Raper, Matthew—Gypsies, Dissertation on the, 4to.
Rarey, J. S.—Taming of Horses.
Rasselas ....*Johnson.*
Rastell, John—Chronicles, 4to., 1811.
Rationalism in Europe ....*Lecky.*
Rattlin the Reefer, with the Three Cutters ....*Marryat.*
Raumer, Fred. von—16th & 17th Centuries, History of, 2 vols.
———— England in 1835, 3 vols.

Raumer, Fred. von—Italy and the Italians, 2 vols.

Ravelin, Humphrey, Lucubrations of

Ravenscliffe, 3 vols.

Rawlinson,G.—Ancient Monarchies of the Eastern World,6 vols.

Ray, J.—Proverbs, Collection of English, 1737.

Raynal, Abbe—Indies, East and West, History of, 8 vols.

Read, C.—Australian Gold Fields, What I heard, saw, & did at

—— Morris—Hand of God in History.

Reade, Charles—Christie Johnson.

———— —— Griffith Gaunt, 3 vols.

——————— Love me little, love me long.

Realities of Irish Life ....*Trench.*

Realmah, 2 vols. ....*Helps.*

Rebellion in 1641, History of the, 7 vols. ....*Clarendon.*

—————— 1745, History of, 4to. ....*Home.*

——————————— Jacobite Memoirs of

————————————— Memoirs of, 4to. ....*De Johnstone.*

Rebellions in Ireland, Memoirs of, 4to. ....*Musgrave.*

Recess, The, a Tour to the Highlands, &c. ....*Johnson.*

Reciprocal Influence of Body and Mind ....*Newnham.*

Reclus, Elisée—Ocean, Atmosphere, and Life, 2 vols.

Recollections of Simeon's Conversation Parties. *A. W. Brown.*

—————— during Reign of George III., 2 vols. ...*Nicholls.*

—————— of the East ....*Carne.*

—————— of a Literary Life, 2 vols. ....*Mitford.*

—————— of a Past Life ....*Holland.*

—————— of a Pedestrian, 3 vols.

—————— of the Peninsula.

Records of the Creation, 2 vols. ....*Sumner.*

Redgauntlet, 3 vols. ....*Scott.*

Redding, Cyrus—Modern Wines, History and Description of

Redgrave, R. and S.—Painters, A Century of, 2 vols.

Redivivus, Thomas B.—Vulgar Errors adapted to 1845.

Reenen, Jacob van—Cape of Good Hope, Journey from, 4to.

Rees, Dr. A.—New Encyclopædia, 84 vols., with Plates, 4to.

—— L. E. R.—Lucknow, Narrative of Siege of

Reeve, Clara—The Old English Baron.

Reformation, History of the, 2 vols. ....*Stebbing.*

——— ——————————— 6 vols. and Index ......*Burnet.*

————— of the 16th Century, History of, 5 vols. *D'Aubigné.*

————— in England, &c., in the time of Calvin. *D'Aubigné.*

Regality, The Glory of ....*Taylor.*

Reginald Dalton, 3 vols. ....,....................*Lockhart.*

Reichenbach, Chas.—Dynamics of Magnetism, Electricity, &c.

Reid, Capt. M.—Odd People.

—— Thomas—Human Mind, Powers of, 3 vols.

——————— Active Powers of Man, Essays on, 4to.

——————— Intellectual Powers of Man, Essays on, 4to.

——————— Ireland, Travels in

——————— Memoirs of, 4to. ....,.*Stewart.*

—— David B.—Ventilation, Theory and Practice of

Reign of Law ....,............*Argyll.*

Reigning Vice, The ....*C. H. Townshend.*

Rein-Deer Dogs and Snow Shoes .... *Bush.*

Rejected Addresses ....*J. and H. Smith.*

—————————— The Genuine

Relhan, Richard—Flora Cantabrigiensis.

Religio Medici, with Observations by Digby ....*Browne.*

Religion, A History of, 2 vols. ....*Evelyn.*

———— of Geology ....*Hitchcock.*

Religions of the World, Lectures on ....*F. D. Maurice.*

Religious Enquiry, The Rationale of ....*J. Martineau.*

———— Idea, On the Development of the ......*Phillipsohn.*

Reliques of Ancient English Poetry, 3 vols. ....*Percy.*

Reliquiæ Diluvianæ; On Organic Remains, 4to. ...*Buckland.*

Remarkable Places, Visits to, 2 vols. ....*Howitt.*

Reminiscences, 2 vols. ....*Kelly.*

——————— ....*Butler.*

Richard III., Historical Doubts on the Reign of, 4to. *Walpole.*
Richards, William—Lynn, History of, 2 vols.
Richardson, Sir J.—Arctic Expedition in Rupert's Land, 2 vols.
———————— The Polar Regions.
————— Robert—Mediterranean, Travels along the, 2 vols.
————— Samuel, Correspondence of, 6 vols. ...*Barbauld.*
——————— Clarissa Harlowe, 8 vols.
——————— Pamela, 4 vols.
——————— Sir Charles Grandison, History of, 7 vols.
Richmond, Rev. Legh, Life of ... .*Grimshawe.*
Richter, Jean Paul F., Life of
Rickman, T.—Architecture in Engld. (Conquest to Reformation).
Ridley, Rev. James—Tales of the Genii, 2 vols.
——— Glocester—Cardinal Pole, Review of Phillips' Life of
Rienzi, a Tragedy, pamphlet ....*Mitford.*
——— 3 vols. ....*Lytton.*
Riesbeck, Baron—Germany, &c., Travels through, 3 vols.
Rifleman, Young, Adventures of a
——— Random Shots from a
Rifleman's Comrade.
Riga to the Crimea, Journey from ....*Holderness.*
Rigby, Edward.—Framingham and its Agriculture, pamphlet.
Riley, James, Captivity of, with Account of Timbuctoo, 4to.
Rimmel, Eugene—Perfumes, Book of
Ring of Amasis, 2 vols. ....*R. B. Lytton.*
Ringstead Abbey, and other Tales ....*Sargant.*
Ripa, Father—Pekin, Residence at Court of
Ritchie, J. E.—Night Side of London.
——— Leitch—Romance of History (France), 3 vols.
River and the Desert, 2 vols. ....*Pardoe.*
Rivers and Torrents, Treatise on, 4to. ....*Frisi.*
Robberds, J. W.—Taylor, Wm., of Norwich, Memoir of, 2 vols.
Roberts, Emma—Bombay, Overland Journey to
——— George—Geology, Dictionary of

Roberts, Mary—Conchologist's Companion.

—— William—More, Hannah, Memoirs of, 4 vols.

Robertson, William, Works of, 8 vols.

———————— America, History of, 4 vols.

———————— Charles V., History of Reign of, 4 vols.

———————— India, Historical Disquisition on, 4to.

———————— Scotland, History of, 2 vols.

———————— Memoirs of, 4to. ....*Stewart.*

Robins, History of the ....*Trimmer.*

Robinson, H. B.—Picton, Sir Thomas, Memoirs of, 2 vols.

—— Henry Crabb, Diary and Correspondence of, 3 vols.

—— Mrs. Mary, Memoirs of, 4 vols. in 2.

—— Nicholas—The Gravel and Stone, Treatise on, 1723.

—— Robert, Life of ....*Dyer.*

—— Crusoe, 2 vols. ....*De Foe.*

Rob-Roy, 3 vols. ....*Scott.*

—— Canoe on the Baltic ....*Macgregor.*

——————————— Jordan .... „

——————— A Thousand Miles in .... „

Rocca, M. de—War of the French in Spain.

Rochefoucault-Liancourt,Ducde—America,TravelsinN.,4vols.

Rock, Capt., Memoirs of

—— Detected.

Rockingham, Sir C.—Cecile, or the Pervert.

——— Marquis of, Memoirs of, 2 vols. *D. of Albemarle.*

Roderick, the Last of the Goths ....*Southey.*

Roger of Wendover—Flowers of History, 2 vols.

Rogers, Henry—*See,* Greyson, R. E. H.

—— Samuel—Human Life.

———————— Italy, a Poem.

———————— Pleasures of Memory.

———————— Recollections.

———————————— of Table Talk of, with Porsoniana.

Roget, P. M.—Physiology, Animal and Vegetable, 2 vols.

Roos, F. F. de—United States of America, Travels in
Ros, Lord de—Tower of London, Memorials of
Rosa, Salvator, Life and Times of, 2 vols. ....*Morgan.*
Rosamond, 2 vols. ....*Edgeworth.*
Rosamund Gray, and Old Blind Margaret ....*Lamb.*
Roscoe, Henry—Lawyers, Eminent British
——— Thomas—Cellini, Benvenuto, Memoirs of, 2 vols.
————— German Novelists, 4 vols.
————— Spain, Tourist in (Andalusia).
————— Silvio Pellico, Memoirs of
————— William the Conqueror, Life of
—— William, Leo the Tenth, Life of, 6 vols.
———————————— & Pontificate of, 2 vols.
————— Lorenzo de Medici, Life of, 2 vols., 4to.
—————————————— Illustrations of, 4to.
————— Life of, 2 vols.
Rose, H. J.—Biographical Dictionary, 12 vols.
—— C. H.—Cats, Book of
—— Hon. Geo.—Fox's Historical Work, Observations on, 4to.
————— Diaries and Correspondence of, 2 vols.
—— W. S.—Italy, Letters from North of, 2 vols.
—— and the Ring ....*Thackeray.*
Rosina, Donna, Memoirs of, 1709.
Ross, Sir J.C.—Antarctic Regions, Voyage of Discovery in, 2 vols.
—— Sir John—Arctic Expedition, Second, 4to.
Rossetti, Dante Gabriel, Poems of
————————— The Early Italian Poets.
Rossini, Signor G., Memoirs of
Rothsay Castle, Wreck of the
Roughing it in the Bush, 2 vols. ....*Moodie.*
Roundabout Papers ....*Thackeray.*
Rousseau, Jean J., Confessions of
Rowe, Nicholas, Poetical Works of, 2 vols.
Rowland, A.—Human Hair popularly & physiologically treated.

Rowton, Frederick—Female Poets of Great Britain.
Royal Society, Transactions of, 1665—1680, 18 vols., 4to.
———————— of New South Wales, Journal, &c., 1878—1880.
Rubens, Sir Peter Paul, His Life and Genius ....*Waagen*.
Ruddiman, Thomas, Life of ....*Chalmers*.
Ruding, Rev. R.—Coinage of Great Britain, 3 vols., 4to.
Rufus, Quintius C.—Alexander the Great, History of, 2 vols.
Rule of Conscience, 1660, folio ....*J. Taylor*.
Rulhiere, M. de—Revolution in Russia in 1762, Anecdotes of
Rumford, Count—Essays, Political, Economical, &c., 3 vols.
———————— Philosophical Papers, vol. i.
Ruminator ; a series of Essays, 2 vols. ....*Brydges*.
Rural Rides ....*Cobbett*.
Rush, Richd.—Court of London, Residence at, 2 series, 3 vols.
Ruskin, John—Stones of Venice, 3 vols.
Russell, Lady Rachel, Letters of, 2 vols.
———————————— Life of
—————— Lord William, Letters and Trial of ...*Lady Russell*.
————————————— Life of, 2 vols. ....*J. Russell*.
—————— Dr.—Modern Europe, History of, 4 vols.
—————— Earl—English Government and Constitution.
——————— Affairs of Europe, On the, 2 vols., 4to.
——————— Fox, Charles J., Memoirs, &c., of, 3 vols.
—————— Rev. M.—Church of Scotland, History of, 2 vols.
——————— Palestine, or the Holy Land.
—————— House of, Memoirs of, 2 vols. ....*Wiffen*.
Russia ....*J. G. Kohl*.
—————— History of, 3 vols.
——————————— 2 vols. ....*Tooke*.
—————— Free, 2 vols. ....*Dixon*.
—————— Travels in, 2 vols. ....*Wilson*.
—————— Biblical Researches and Travels in ....*Henderson*.
—————— Revelations of, 2 vols.
—————— Expedition to, 2 vols. ....*Segur*.

Russia, Campaign in, 4to. ....*Porter.*
——————————— ....*Labaume.*
—— on the Black Sea and Sea of Azof ....*Seymour.*
—— in the East, Progress and Present Position of
—— Military and Political Power of, in 1817 ......*Wilson.*
—— and the War ....*Jesse.*
—— and the Russians in 1842, 2 vols. ....*Kohl.*
—— and Sweden, Courts of, 2 vols. ....*Frankland.*
—— and Tartary, Journey through, 2 vols. ......*Cochrane.*
Russian Army, On the Character of ....*Wilson.*
—— Empire, Anecdotes of
——————— View of, 3 vols. ....*Tooke.*
—— Sheep, Account of ....*Pallas.*
—— Shores of the Black Sea ....*Oliphant.*
Russians of the South ....*Brooks.*
Ruth, 3 vols. ....*Gaskell.*
Rutherford, William—Ancient History, View of, 2 vols.
Rutter, J. O. N.—Human Electricity.
Ruxton, Geo. F.—Mexico & Rocky Mountains, Adventures in
Ryan, Richard—Dramatic Table Talk, 3 vols.

SABBATH, The, and other Poems ....*Graham.*
——————— Sundry Tracts on
Sabrinæ Corolla ; English Poetry, rendered into Greek & Latin.
Sacred and Legendary Art ....*Jameson.*
—— History of the World, 3 vols. ....*Turner.*
—— Mountains, The ....*Headley.*
—— Poems.
——————— for Mourners ; Introduction by Archbp. Trench.
—— Poetry, Collection of
Sailor, Life of a, 3 vols.
Sailor's Yarn, A ....*Wigston.*
Saint Fond, B. F.—England and Scotland, Travels in, 2 vols.
—— Priest, A. de—Jesuits, History of the Fall of

Saint's Tragedy ....*C. Kingsley, Junr.*
Sala, George Augustus—Gaslight and Daylight.
Sale, Lady—Afghanistan, Journal of Disasters in
—— George—Koran, with Explanatory Notes, 2 vols.
Salkeld, John—Angels, Treatise on, 1613.
Salmagundi ....*Irving.*
Salmon, J.—Rome, Antiquities of, 2 vols.
—— Fishing in the Tweed, Days and Nights of ...*Scrope.*
Salmonia, or Days of Salmon Fishing.
Salt, Henry, Life and Correspondence of, 2 vols. ......*Halls.*
—— the Forbidden Food ....*Howard.*
Salter, Joseph—Asiatic in England.
Samor, Lord of the Bright City ....*Milman.*
Sancho, or the Proverbialist.
Sancroft, Archbishop, Life of, 2 vols. ....*D'Oyly.*
Sandby, George—Mesmerism and its Opponents.
Sandford and Merton ....*Day.*
Sandwith, Humphrey—Kars, Narrative of Siege of
Sarawak, Ten Years in ....*Brooke.*
Sardanapalus, with Two Foscari, and Cain, 1821.
Sargant, J. A.—Cranmer, Archbishop, Life of
—————— Ringstead Abbey, and other Tales.
Saulcy, F. de—Dead Sea, Journey round, 2 vols.
Savage Club Papers for 1868 ....*Halliday.*
Savary, Mons.—Greece, Letters on
————— Egypt, Letters on, 2 vols.
Savigny, J. B. H.—Medusa Frigate, Account of the Loss of
Savings, Annals of Banks for
Sayings and Doings, 3 series, 9 vols.
Scarborough, Journal of a Tour to, 1798 ....*Hutchesson.*
Scarlet Letter, The ....*Hawthorne.*
Scarron, Mons., Comical Works of, 1700.
Scenes and Impressions in Egypt.
————— Tales of Country Life ....*Jesse.*

Scott, Sir Walter—Lord of the Isles.
——————————— Marmion.
——————————— Minstrelsy of the Scottish Border, 3 vols.
——————————— Rokeby.
——————————— Sir Tristrem.
——————————— Vision of Don Roderick.
——————————— Abbot, The
——————————— Anne of Geierstein.
——————————— Antiquary.
——————————— Betrothed, The
——————————— Black Dwarf.
——————————— Bride of Lammermoor.
——————————— Castle Dangerous.
——————————— Chronicles of the Canongate, 2 series, 5 vols.
——————————— Count Robert of Paris.
——————————— Crusaders, Tales of the, 4 vols.
——————————— Fair Maid of Perth.
——————————— Fortunes of Nigel.
——————————— Guy Mannering.
——————————— Heart of Mid-Lothian.
——————————— Highland Widow.
——————————— Ivanhoe.
——————————— Kenilworth.
——————————— Legend of Montrose.
——————————— Monastery, The
——————————— Old Mortality.
——————————— Peveril of the Peak.
——————————— Pirate, The
——————————— Quentin Durward.
——————————— Redgauntlet.
——————————— Rob Roy.
——————————— St. Ronan's Well.
——————————— Surgeon's Daughter.
——————————— Tales of My Landlord, 4 series, 4 vols. ea.

Scott, Sir Walter—Talisman, The
———————— Waverley.
———————— Woodstock.
———————— Memoirs of the Life of, 7 vols. ...*Lockhart.*
Scottish Gael, 2 vols. ....*Logan.*
——— Life, Lights and Shadows of ....*Wilson.*
Scrap Book, Juvenile, 1838 ....*B. Barton.*
Scratchley, Arthur—Life Assurance, &c., Observations on
Scripture Texts, arranged under heads, 4to. (wants title.)
——— Canon of, Scholastical History of, fcap. 4to. *Cosin.*
Scriptures, Holy; in English, French, German, Latin, & Greek.
Scrope, Wm.—Deer Stalking, Art of
———————— Salmon Fishing in the Tweed, Days & Nights of
Sea Lions ....*Cooper.*
Seaman, Autobiography of a ....*Dundonald.*
Search after Proserpine, and other Poems ....*De Vere.*
Season Ticket, The
Seaward, Sir Edw.—Narrative of his Shipwreck, 3 vols. *Porter.*
Sebastopol, A Month in the Camp before
Second Love ....*Mrs. Trollope.*
Secret History of Charles II., 2 vols.
——— Memoirs of the Court of St. Petersburg, 3 vols.
Secrets of Art and Nature, 4to., 1660 ....*Wecker.*
Sedgwick, Prof. Adam—University of Cambridge, On Studies of
——— Miss—Letters from Abroad, 2 vols.
Seely, John B.—Elora, Wonders of
Seeman, Berthold—H.M.S. Herald, Voyage of, 1845—1851.
Segur, Count—Russia, Expedition to, 2 vols.
Seine, Moselle, &c., Steam Voyage on ....*Quin.*
Self, by the Author of Cecil.
—— Control, 3 vols.
—— Help ....*Smiles.*
Selkirk, Earl of—On Emigration.
Selwyn, George, and his Contemporaries, 4 vols. ......*Jesse.*

Shakespeare, Wm.—Poems, 1774.

———————————— Notes & Lectures on..*Mrs.H.W.Coleridge.*

———————————— Sentiments and Similes of ...*Humphreys.*

———————————— Sonnets of, Fac-simile of edition 1609.

Sharp, Granville, Memoirs of, 2 vols. ....*Prince Hoare.*

——— Richard—Letters and Essays.

——— S.—Surgery, Treatise on Operations of, 1739.

——————————— Critical inquiry into Present State of,1750.

Shaw, Col. C., Memoirs and Correspondence of, 2 vols.

——— George—Zoological Lectures, 2 vols.

——— Peter—Chemistry, New Method of, 4to., 1727.

————— Dispensatory, Edinburgh, 1727.

————— Physic, New Practice of, vol. i., 1730.

Shee, Sir M. A., P.R.A.—Reynolds, Sir J., Commemoration of

Sheeraz, Tour to, 4to. ....*Waring.*

Sheffield, Lord J.—American States, On the Commerce of,1784.

Sheil, Lady—Persia, Glimpses of Life and Manners in

——— Richard Lalor—Evadne, a Tragedy.

——————————— Sketches, Legal and Political

——————————— Later Memoirs of ....*Mc Cullagh.*

Shelley, Mrs.—Germany,France,&c., Rambles in,1842-3,2 vols.

——— Percy Bysshe, Poetical Works of, 3 vols.

——————————— Relics of

——————————— Memorials of ....*Lady Shelley.*

——————————— Life of, 2 vols. ....*Hogg.*

——————————— and Byron, Last Days of ...*Trelawney.*

Shells, Manual of British ....*Turton.*

Shenstone, William, Poetical Works of, 1797.

——————————— Some Particulars in the Life of

Shepherd, Rev. William—Paris in 1802 and 1814.

Shepherd's Calendar ....*Clare.*

Sheridan, Richard Brinsley, Speeches of, 3 vols.

——————————— Works of, 2 vols.

——————————— Life of, 2 vols. ....*Watkins.*

Sotheby, Wm.—Oberon, from the German of Wieland, 2 vols.

Soul, The, her Sorrows and her Aspirations ....*Newman.*

South Pole, Voyage towards ....*Weddell.*

—— Sea, Voyage of Discovery in, 3 vols. ....*Kotzebue.*

——— Islands, Missionary Enterprises in ......*Williams.*

—————— Voyages, &c., in, 2 vols. *Tyerman & Bennet.*

—— Seas, Visit to ....*Stewart.*

Southey, Robert—Book of the Church, 2 vols.

—————— British Admirals, Biography of, 5 vols.

——————— Battles.

————— Bunyan and Cromwell, Lives of

————— Colloquies on the Progress of Society, 2 vols.

————— Common Place Book, 4 vols.

————— Curse of Kehama.

————— Doctor, The

————— Joan of Arc.

————— Lay of the Laureates.

————— Letters of, Selection from

————— from Spain and Portugal.

————— Love Story, A

————— Madoc.

————— Minor Poems, 3 vols.

————— Nelson, Lord, Life of, 2 vols.

————— Oliver Newman.

————— Orsua, &c., Expedition of

————— Omniana, 2 vols.

————— Peninsular War, History of, 3 vols., 4to.

————— Political Works.

————— Poet's Pilgrimage to Waterloo.

————— Poetical Works, 10 vols.

————— Roderick, the Last of the Goths, 2 vols.

————— Tale of Paraguay.

————— Thalaba, or the Destroyer.

————— Wesley, John, Life of, 2 vols.

Southey, Robert, Life of ....*Brown.*
————-————— & Correspondence, 6 vols. *C.C.Southey.*
Southgate, Henry—Many Thoughts on Many Things, 4to.
Southwold, Topographical Description of
Soyer, Alexis—Culinary Campaign.
Spain, History of, 3 vols.
—— Gatherings from ....*Ford.*
—— Journey through, 2 vols., 4to. ....*Townshend.*
————-————— 2 vols. ....*Semple.*
—— Second Journey in ...., „
—— in 1830, 2 vols. ....*Inglis.*
—— A Year in, 2 vols.
-—— Bourbon Kings of, Memoirs of, 5 vols. ....*Coxe.*
—— and the Spaniards in 1843, 2 vols. ......*Widdrington.*
—— British Army in, Campaign of ....*Moore.*
-—— War of the Succession in ·..........................*Mahon.*
————————French in, Memoir of the ......*De Rocca.*
—— South, Travels in, 4to. ....*Jacob.*
—— and France, Forced Journey through, 2 vols. *Blaney.*
————— Portugal, War in, Account of ....*Jones.*
——————— Letters from ....*Southey.*
——————— History of, 5 vols.
——————— and Italy, with Vathek ....*Beckford.*
Spalding, Gentlemen's Society at, Account of, 4to.
Spallanzani, Abbe—Natural History, Dissertations on, 2 vols.
———————————-—— of Animals, &c., 2 vols.
——————— Two Sicilies, Travels in, 4 vols.
Spanish Ballads ....*Lockhart.*
—— Gypsy ....*Eliot.*
—— Revolution, Historical Review of ....*Blaquiere.*
Sparks from the Anvil ....*Burritt.*
Sparrman, Andrew—Cape of Good Hope, Voyage to, 2 vols., 4to.
Spas of England, 3 vols. ....*Granville.*
—— Germany, 2 vols. .... „

Spectator, The, edited by Chalmers, 6 vols.
Speke, J. H.—Nile, Discovery of the Source of
Spence, Rev. Joseph—Anecdotes of Books and Men.
———— Eliz. I.—Scotland, Sketches of Manners, &c., of, 2 vols.
Spencer, Edmund—Circassia, &c., Travels in, 2 vols.
———————— European Turkey, Travels in, 2 vols.
———— Rev. G. T.—Journal of a Visitation Tour.
Spenser, Edmund, Works of, by Todd, 8 vols.
————————— Life and Poetical Works of, 5 vols.
Spicer, Henry—Sights and Sounds.
Spiker, Dr. S. H.—England, Wales, & Scotland, Travels thro'
Spirit of the Age ....*Hazlitt.*
———— Giant Mountains, and other Tales.
—— Manifestations ....*Ballou.*
Spirits, Relation of his Action with, folio, 1659 ....*Dee.*
Spiritual Quixote, 3 vols.
———— Teacher; Lectures by Spirits of the 6th circle. *Ambler.*
———— Wives, 2 vols. ....*Dixon.*
Spiritualism ....*Crowe.*
Spy, The ....*Cooper.*
Squirrell, Elizabeth, Autobiography of
St. Augustine, Confessions of, 1679.
— Clair, Lady H.—Dainty Dishes.
— Helena, History of ....*Brooke.*
———— Letters from ....*Warden.*
———— Tracts relative to the Island of, 4to. ......*Beatson.*
———— Bonaparte at, Treatment of
— John, J. H.—British Colonies, Letters on
———— Bayle—Two Years' Residence in a Levantine Family.
———— Charles—Wild Sports of the Highlands.
———— Mrs. H.—Audubon; The Naturalist in the New World.
———— J. A.—Margaret Ravenscroft.
— Julian.
— Leon, 4 vols. ....*Godwin.*

St. Luke, Essay on the Writings of ....*Schleiermacher.*
— Paul, Life and Epistles of, 2 vols. *Conybeare and Howson.*
————— Continuous History of ....*Tape.*
————— Essays on the Writings of ....*Whateley.*
— Peter, Lectures on ....,.........*Blunt.*
— Petersburg, Travels to and from, 2 vols. ....*Granville.*
—————— Visit to ....*Raikes.*
—————— Secret Memoirs of the Court of
— Phale, Mdlle. de, History of, 1758.
— Pierre, Bernardin de—Paul and Virginia.
— Ronan's Well ....*Scott.*
— Vincent, Earl of, Memoirs of, 2 vols. ....*Tucker.*
Stackhouse, Thomas—History of Bible, 2 vols., folio, 1733.
Staël, Madame de—French Revolution, Considerations on, 3 vols.
—————— Germany, 3 vols.
—————— Necker, Life of, and Miscellanies by
—————— Life and Times of ....*Norris.*
—————— Sketch of Life and Writings of
—————— and the Grand Duchess Louise.
Stamford, History of ....*Drakard.*
Stanhope, Lady Hester, Travels of, 3 vols.
—————————— Memoirs, 3 vols.
Stanley, Dean—Arnold, Dr. T., Life & Correspondence of, 2 vols.
—————— Eastern Church, Lectures on
————— Jewish Church, Lectures on, 2 vols.
—————— Sinai and Palestine.
—————— Westminster Abbey, Memorials of
——— Bishop—Birds, Familiar History of
State Medicine, Lectures on ....*Elliotson.*
—— Papers, 2 vols., 4to. .... *Macpherson.*
—————— of John Thurloe, by Birch, 7 vols., folio.
—— Trials, 1163—1820, 34 vols. ....*Cobbett.*
————— Modern, 2 vols. ....*Townsend.*
Statesmen of Commonwealth, 5 vols. ....*Forster.*

Strang, John—Germany in 1831, 2 vols.

Strange Story, A ....*Lytton.*

Stratford-upon-Avon, Account of

Strauss, Dr. D. F.—Christ, Life of, 3 vols.

Stream of Life on our Globe ....*J. L. Milton.*

Strickland, Agnes—Queens of England, 12 vols.

———————————————— Scotland,8vols.(vol.v.missing).

————————— Mary, Queen of Scots, Letters of, 3 vols.

————— Major—Canada,West,27years' Residence in,2vols.

Strife and Peace ....*Bremer.*

Struensee, Count, Conversion and Death of

Stuart, Gilbert—Scotland, History of, 2 vols.

————— Society in Europe, View of, 4to.

——— Rev. A. M.—Last Duchess of Gordon, Life & Letters of

——— Andrew—Letters to Lord Mansfield, 4to.

——— Jas.—America, Three Years' Residence in North,2vols.

——— of Dunleath ....*Mrs. Norton.*

Student, The, 2 vols. ....*Lytton.*

Sturkey, H. G.—Heir of Maberley, 2 vols.

Sturt, Capt. C.—Australia, Expedition into Central, 2 vols.

Subaltern, The

Subtle Brains and Lissom Fingers ....*Wynter.*

Suckling, Sir John—Collection of Incomparable Pieces, 1658.

Sully, Duke of, Memoirs of, 6 vols.

Sumatra, History of, 4to. ....*Marsden.*

Sumner, Archbishop—Creation, Records of the, 2 vols.

Sun, Spots on the, Observations of ....*Carrington.*

——— Moon, and Stars, Tales about the ...(*P. Parley*) *Goodrich.*

Sunday in London ....*Capes.*

————————— illustrated by Cruikshank.

Sunny Memories of Foreign Lands, 2 vols. ....*Stowe.*

Surgeon, The Complete, 1727 ....*Le Clerc.*

Surgery, Art of, 2 vols., 1725 ....*Turner.*

————————— Appendix to, 1725 ....   ,,

Swift, Dean, Life and Works of, 19 vols. ....*Scott.*
———————————————— 17 vols. ....*Sheridan.*
Swinburne, Hy.—Courts of Europe, close of last century, 2 vols.
——————— Two Sicilies, Travels in, 2 vols., 4to.
————Algernon—Poems and Ballads.
Swiss Guide, Practical
Switzerland, History of
——————— Village Life in ....*Delmard.*
—————— Tour and Residence in, 2 vols. ....*Simond.*
—————— and Italy, Letters from ....*Carne.*
—————— and South of France ....*Inglis.*
Switzers, The, 2 vols. ....*Dixon.*
Sybil ....*B. D'Israeli.*
Sydenham, Lord Charles, Memoirs of
Sylva, or the Wood ; a Collection of Anecdotes.
—— Florifera, 2 vols. ....*Phillips.*
Sylvia, or the May Queen ....*Darley.*
Symmons, Charles—Milton, John, Life of
Synonyms, English, Collection of
Syntax, Dr., 3 Tours of, 3 vols., illus. by Rowlandson. *W. Combe.*
Syria and Egypt, Travels in, 2 vols. ....*Volney.*
——————— the Holy Land ....*Burckhardt.*
——— Summer Ramble in, 2 vols. ....*Monro.*
Syrian Churches, Early History of ....*Etheridge.*
——————— Recension of the Four Gospels, Remains of ...*Cureton.*
Szyrma, Col. Lach—Siberia, Revelations of, 2 vols.

TABLE Talk, or Original Essays, 2 vols. ....*Hazlitt.*
——————— of S. T. Coleridge, Specimens of, 2 vols.
——————— of S. Rogers, Recollections of, with Porsoniana.
Tacitus, Cornelius, Works of, by Murphy, 8 vols.
Tait's Edinburgh Magazine for 1836.
Talbot, Mrs. Catherine, Works of
——— Chas., Earl of Shrewsbury, Correspondence of, 4to. *Coxe.*

Tale Book, 2 vols.

—— of Two Cities ....*Dickens.*

—— of a Tub, with Notes, 1727 ....*Swift.*

Tales, Original, 2 vols. ....*Cumberland.*

—— of Fashionable Life, 6 vols. ....*Edgeworth.*

———— Old Japan, 2 vols. ....*Mitford.*

———— Wonder, and other Poems ....*Lewis.*

———— a Traveller, 2 vols. ....*Irving.*

———— a Wayside Inn .... *Longfellow.*

———— My Landlord, 4 series, 4 vols. each ....*Scott.*

———— the Castle, 5 vols. ....*Holcroft.*

———— the Hall, 2 vols. ....*Crabbe.*

———— the Wars of our Times, 2 vols.

———— the West, 2 vols.

—— from Denmark ....*Andersen.*

—— from the German.

—— and Poems ....*Lytton.*

Talfourd, F. N.—Charles Lamb, Letters of

——————————————— Final Memorials of

———————— Ion, Athenian Captive, Glencoe.

———————— The Castilian, a Poem.

———————— Tragedies.

———————— Vacation Rambles and Thoughts, 2 vols.

—————————————— &c., Supplement to

Talisman, The ....*Scott.*

Talleyrand, Prince, Life of, 4 vols.

——————— Memoirs of

Tancred ....*B. D'Israeli.*

Tannhaüser, a Poem ....*Temple and Trevor.*

Tape, James—St. Paul, Continuous History of

Tasmania, My Home in ....*Meredith.*

Tasso, Torquato—Jerusalem Delivered, trans. by Hoole, 2 vols.

——————————————— trans. by Fairfax, 2 vols. in 1.

Taste, Essays on, 4to. ....*Alison.*

Thackeray, Wm. M., the Humourist & Man of Letters. *Taylor.*
———— ———— English Humourists of the 18th Century.
———— ———— Miscellanies, 4 vols.
———— ———— Ballads and Tales.
———— ———— Book of Snobs.
———— ———— Burlesques.
———— ———— Catherine.
———— ———— Christmas Books.
———— ———— Denis Duval, Lovel the Widower, &c.
———— ———— Esmond.
———— ———— Four Georges.
———— ———— Irish Sketch Book.
———— ———— Kickleburys on the Rhine.
———— ———— Newcomes, The, 2 vols.
———— ———— Paris Sketch Book, &c.
———— ———— Pendennis, 2 vols.
———— ———— Philip, Adventures of, 2 vols.
———— ———— Rose and the Ring.
———— ———— Roundabout Papers.
———— ———— Titmarsh, Samuel, History of
———— ———— Vanity Fair, 2 vols.
———— ———— Virginians, The, 2 vols.
Thalaba, the Destroyer ....*Southey.*
Thames and its Tributaries, 2 vols. ....*Mackay.*
Thankfulness, a Narrative ....*Tayler.*
Theatres of Paris ....*Hervey.*
Theatrical Inquisitor, 1812—1820, 16 vols.
Theodric, and other Poems ....*Campbell.*
Theological Essays ....*Maurice.*
Theory of Life ....*S. T. Coleridge.*
Thespian Dictionary, 1805.
Thibet and China, Travels in ....*Huc.*
——— Tartary, &c., Social and Political Condition of *Prinsep.*
Thieme, F. W.—Dictionary, English and German

Timbs, John—Curiosities of London.
———— English Eccentrics and Eccentricities, 2 vols.
———— Knowledge for the Times.
———— London and Westminster, 2 vols.
———— Romance of London, 3 vols.
———— Strange Stories of the Animal World.
———— Things not generally known.
———— Walks and Talks about London.
Timbuctoo, Captivity and Residence at, 4to. ....*Adams.*
———————— in the Desert and Account of, 4to. *Riley.*
———— and Housa, Account of ....*Jackson.*
Time the Avenger.
Times, Estimate of the Manners of the, 2 vols., 1758. *Brown.*
Tin Trumpet, The, 2 vols. ....*P. Chatfield.*
Tinseau, Chevalier de—France, Statistical View of, 1803.
Tinsley's Magazine, 1868 to 1880.
Tippoo Sultaun, View of the War with, 4to. ....*Beatson.*
Titmarsh, Samuel, History of ....*Thackeray.*
Tobacco, A Pipe of, and Pandora's Box.
Tobin, J. J.—Italy, &c., Tour in
Tocqueville, Alexis de—Democracy in America, 4 vols.
———————— Memoir, Letters and Remains of
———————— Society in France bef. Revolution 1798.
Todd, Rev. H. J.—Milton, John, Life and Writings of
Tom Brown's School Days ....*Hughes.*
—— Cringle's Log ....*M. Scott.*
—— Jones, 3 vols., 1780 ....*Fielding.*
—— Rocket ....*Fonblanque.*
Tomline, Bishop—Pitt, Rt. Hon. Wm., Life of, vols. i. & ii., 4to.
Tonga Islands, Account of, 2 vols. ....*Martin.*
——————————— Natives of, 2 vols. ......*Mariner.*
Tooke, J. Horne—Diversions of Purley, 2 vols.
———— William—Russia, History of, 2 vols.
———————— Russian Empire, View of, 3 vols.

Traveller's Oracle, 2 vols. ....*Kitchener.*
Travelling Memoranda, 1786—1788, 2 vols. ......*Gardenstone.*
Travels in the Air ....*Glaisher.*
Travis, George—Letters to Edward Gibbon.
Trelawney, E. J.—Shelley and Byron, Last Days of
Tremaine, or the Man of Refinement, 3 vols.
Tremenheere, H. S.—Notes on Public Subjects.
Trench, Archbishop—English, Past and Present
——————————— Miracles, Notes on
——————————— Parables, Notes on
——————————— Poems.
——————————— Genoveva, a Poem.
—————— Mrs. Richard, Remains of
—————— W. S.—Realities of Irish Life.
Trenck, Baron, Autobiography of, trans. from German, 2 vols.
Trevelyan ....*Lady Bury.*
Trevlyn Hold ....*Mrs. H. Wood.*
Trials, Remarkable, Reports of, vol. i. ....*Craik.*
——————————— in Great Britain.
——————————— Criminal ....*Feuerbach.*
Trifles, or Friendly Mites for Youth, 1800.
Trimmer, Mrs.—History of the Robins.
—————— —— Miscellaneous Pieces.
——————— Life and Writings of, 2 vols.
Tripoli, Ten Years' Residence at, 4to. ....*Tully.*
Tristram, Canon H. B.—Land of Moab.
Trollope, Anthony—Barchester Towers, 3 vols.
——————————— Can you forgive her ? 2 vols.
————— —— ——— Doctor Thorne.
——————————— Last Chronicle of Barset, 2 vols.
·——————————— Orley Farm, 2 vols.
——————————— West Indies and the Spanish Main.
—————— Mrs.—Americans, Domestic Manners of, 2 vols.
——————— Belgium & Western Germany in 1833, 2 vols.

WAAGEN, Dr.—Art Treasures in Great Britain, 3 vols.
——————— Galleries & Cabinets of Art in Great Britain.
——————— Rubens, P. P., Life and Genius of
Wagner, Dr. F., & F. Bodenstedt—Schamyl of the Caucasus.
Wakefield, Edward—Ireland, Account of, 2 vols., 4to.
——————— Edward J.—New Zealand, Adventures in, 2 vols.
Waldegrave, Lord, Memoirs of, 1745—1758, 4to.
Waldenses, and other Poems ....*De Vere.*
Waldensian Researches in Piedmont, 2 vols. ....*Gilly.*
Wales, The Worthiness of, 1776 ....*Churchyard.*
——————— History of, 4to. ....*Warrington.*
——————— North, Tour through ....*Aikin.*
Walford, Edward—Prince Consort, Life of
Walker, Thomas—The Original.
Walker's Universal Atlas.
Wallace, Alfred R.—Amazon and River Negro, Travels on
——————————— Malay Archipelago, 2 vols.
——————— a Metrical Romance ....*Holford.*
Wallachia and Moldavia, Account of ....*Wilkinson.*
Wallenstein, Count Albrecht, Life of ....*Mitchell.*
Waller, Edmund—Poems.
Walpole, Hon. F.—The Ansayrii ; Travels in the East, 2 vols.
——————— Horace—Castle of Otranto, 1791.
——————————— George III., Journal of Reign of, 2 vols.
——————————— Horace Mann, Letters to, 2 series, 7 vols.
——————————— Private Correspondence of, 4 vols.
——————————— Richard III., Historical Doubts on Reign of
——————————— Royal and Noble Authors, 2 vols., 1757.
——————— Rev. Robert—Travels in the East, 4to.
——————————— Turkey, Memoirs on, 4to.
——————— Sir Robert, Memoirs of, 3 vols., 4to. ....*Coxe.*
Walrond, T.—James, 8th Earl of Elgin, Letters & Journals of
Walsh, Rev. R.—Coins, Medals, and Gems, Essay on
——————— Constantinople to England, Journey from

Wellington, Duke of, Life of, 3 vols. ....*Maxwell.*
——————— Memoir of
Wells, William Charles—Dew, Essay on
—— Samuel—Bedford Level, History of Drainage of, 2 vols.
Wellwood, J. M.—Erskine, John, Life and Writings of
Wendeborn, Fred. A.—England, View of, 2 vols.
Wentworth, W. C.—New South Wales, Description of
Were-Wolves, Book of ....*Baring-Gould.*
Werner, a Tragedy ....*Byron.*
Wesley, John, Life of, 2 vols. ....*Southey.*
West, Benjamin, P.R.A., Life of, 2 vols. ....*Galt.*
—— Mrs. Jane—Letters to a Young Lady, 3 vols.
———————————————— Man, 3 vols.
Western Empire, History of, 2 vols. ....*Comyn.*
——— World in 1846, 1847, 3 vols. ....*Mackay.*
————— (United States), History of, 2 vols.
Westminster Abbey, Memorials of ....*Stanley.*
————— Ancient Palace of, History of *Brayley & Britton.*
Westward Ho ! ....*Kingsley.*
Wetherell, Elizabeth—Queechy.
——————— Wide, Wide World.
Whaling Voyage round the Globe, 2 vols. ....*Bennett.*
What will he do with it ? 4 vols. ....*Lytton.*
Whateley, Archbishop—Bacon's Essays, with Annotations.
————————— Christian Religion, Essays on
————————— Kingdom of Christ.
——————— Logic, Elements of
——————— St. Paul, On the Writings of
——— M. L.—Among the Huts in Egypt.
Wheatley, H. B.—On Anagrams.
Wheeler, William—Noted Names of Fiction, Dictionary of
Whewell, Rev. W.—Architectural Notes on German Churches.
————— Astronomy and General Physics.
Whim and its Consequences.

Wisbech Literary Society, Catalogue of Books, 1836, 1849.
——— Historical Account of ....*Col. Watson.*
——— History of ....*Watson and Craddock.*
——— Introduction to the Charter of, 4to. ......*Hutchesson.*
Wiseman, Richard—Surgical Treatises, folio, 1686.
Wit and Humour ....*Hood.*
Witchcraft, History of, 2 vols. .:............................*Locke.*
——— ——— Historical Essay on, 1718 ....*Hutchinson.*
——— ——— Philosophy of ....*Mitchell and Dickie.*
Witches and Apparitions, Evidence concerning, 1726. *Glanville.*
Wives of England ....*Ellis.*
Wolcott, Dr. John, (Peter Pindar)—Poems, 3 vols., 4to.
Wolff, Dr. Joseph—Bokhara, Mission to, 2 vols.
——— ——— ——— Travels and Adventures of, 2 vols.
Wolsey, Cardinal, Life and Administration of ....*Galt.*
Wollstonecraft, Mary—Rights of Women, Vindication of, vol. i.
——— ——— ——— Norway, Sweden, &c., Letters on
Woman, 3 vols.
——— A Vindication of the Rights of, vol. i. *Wollstonecraft.*
——— in France during 18th Century, 2 vols. ...*Kavanagh.*
——— in White ....*Collins.*
Woman's, A, Journey round the World ....*Ida Pfeiffer.*
Women, History of, 2 vols., 4to. ....*Alexander.*
——— Characteristics of, 2 vols. ....*Jameson.*
——— of England ....*Ellis.*
Wood, J. G.—Homes without Hands.
——— Mrs. Henry—Lady Lisle.
——— ——— ——— Mrs. Halliburton's Troubles.
——— ——— ——— Oswald Cray.
——— ——— ——— Trevlyn Hold.
Woodfall, W.—Register or Diary, folio, 1791.
Woodhouse, James—Poems.
Woodman, The ....*James.*
Woodreve Manor ....*Dorsey.*

BOOKS IN OTHER LANGUAGES.

FRENCH.

ABOUT, E.—Germaine.
———————— La Question Romaine.
———————— Le Cas de Monsieur Guérin.
———————— L'Homme à l'Oreille Cassée.
———————— Le Nez d'un Notaire.
———————— Les Mariages de Paris.
———————— Madélon.
Achard, A.—Nelly.
Adèle et Théodore, ou Lettres sur l'Education.
Aimard, G.—L'Araucan.
Alexandre, C.—Dictionnaire Grec—Francais.
Almanach de Gotha, 1866, 1867, 2 vols.
———————— des Muses, 1776.
Amis de Madame, Les
Amour et Diplomatie.
Andersen, H.—Contes, traduits du Danois.
Arago, F.—Leçons d'Astronomie.
Arnin, A. d'—Contes Bizarres.
Assolant, A.—D'Heure en Heure.
Aubryet, X.—La Femme de Vingt-cinq Ans.
Audouard, Madame—Les Mystères de l'Egypte devoilés.
Aurevilly, J. Barbey d'—L'Amour Impossible.
———————————————— L'Ensorcelée.

BALZAC, H. de—Balthazar Claës ou la Récherche de l'Absolu.
———————————— Eugénie Grandet.

BALZAC, H. de—La Peau de Chagrin.
———————— Le Cousin Pons ou les deux Musiciens, 2 vols.
———————— Le Père Goriot.
———————— Pierrette.
Barthélemy, J. J.—Carite et Polydore, 1799.
Bazancourt, Baron de—Un Dernier Souvenir.
Beauchesne, A. de—Louis XVII. ; sa vie, son agonie, sa mort.
Beauregard, C. de—Mémoires Historiques sur la Maison de Savoie.
Beauvoir, Madame de—Confidences de Mademoiselle Mars.
Bellot, J. R.—Journal d'un Voyage aux mers polaires.
Beranger, P. J. de—Ma Biographie.
———————— Œuvres de, 3 vols.
Bernard, C. de—Gerfaut.
———————— Le Gentilhomme Campagnard, 2 vols.
———————— Le Paravent.
Berthet, E.—La Belle Drapière.
Berton, Caroline—Rosette.
Blanchet, R.—Lausanne, dès les temps anciens, 1863.
Boccard, M.—Histoire du Vallais.
Boileau, N.—Œuvres de, 4 vols., 1729.
Bois de Boulogne et ses Environs.
Bonnet, Chas.—Œuvres d'Histoire Naturelle, 8 vols., 4to., 1779.
Bossuet, J. B.—Collection Complète des Sermons, 17 vols., 1808.
Bouilli, J. N.—Contes à ma fille, 2 vols.
Bourdaloue, Louis, Œuvres de, 16 vols.
Braddon, Miss—La Trace du Serpent (traduction), 2 vols.
Bravard, R.—L'Honneur des Femmes.
———————— Une Petite Ville.
Bréhat, A.—Histoires d'Amour.
———————— Les Amoureux de Vingt Ans.
———————— Les Jeunes Amours.
Bressant, Alix—Gabriel Pinson.
———————— Une Paria.
Brunet, J. C.—Manuel du Libraire, 5 vols.

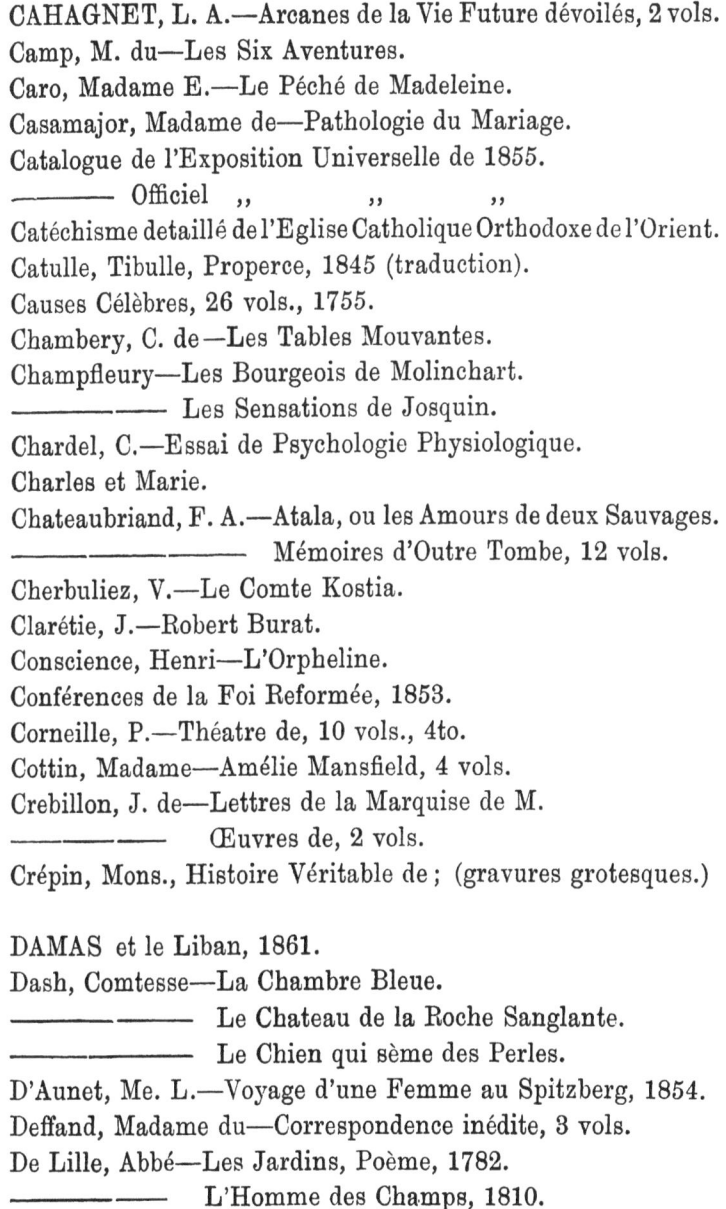

CAHAGNET, L. A.—Arcanes de la Vie Future dévoilés, 2 vols.
Camp, M. du—Les Six Aventures.
Caro, Madame E.—Le Péché de Madeleine.
Casamajor, Madame de—Pathologie du Mariage.
Catalogue de l'Exposition Universelle de 1855.
———— Officiel ,, ,, ,,
Catéchisme detaillé de l'Eglise Catholique Orthodoxe de l'Orient.
Catulle, Tibulle, Properce, 1845 (traduction).
Causes Célèbres, 26 vols., 1755.
Chambery, C. de—Les Tables Mouvantes.
Champfleury—Les Bourgeois de Molinchart.
———————— Les Sensations de Josquin.
Chardel, C.—Essai de Psychologie Physiologique.
Charles et Marie.
Chateaubriand, F. A.—Atala, ou les Amours de deux Sauvages.
————————————— Mémoires d'Outre Tombe, 12 vols.
Cherbuliez, V.—Le Comte Kostia.
Clarétie, J.—Robert Burat.
Conscience, Henri—L'Orpheline.
Conférences de la Foi Reformée, 1853.
Corneille, P.—Théatre de, 10 vols., 4to.
Cottin, Madame—Amélie Mansfield, 4 vols.
Crebillon, J. de—Lettres de la Marquise de M.
————————— Œuvres de, 2 vols.
Crépin, Mons., Histoire Véritable de ; (gravures grotesques.)

DAMAS et le Liban, 1861.
Dash, Comtesse—La Chambre Bleue.
————————— Le Chateau de la Roche Sanglante.
————————— Le Chien qui sème des Perles.
D'Aunet, Me. L.—Voyage d'une Femme au Spitzberg, 1854.
Deffand, Madame du—Correspondence inédite, 3 vols.
De Lille, Abbé—Les Jardins, Poème, 1782.
————————— L'Homme des Champs, 1810.

Demoustier—Lettres à Emilie sur la Mythologie, vols. iii. & iv.

Devique, E.—Les Mères Coupables.

Dickens, Chas.—Le Magazin d'Antiquités, (traduction), 2 vols.

————— Les Contes de Noël, (traduction.)

————— Les Temps Difficiles,   ,,

————— Nicolas Nickleby, Vie de, (traduction), 2 vols.

Dictionnaire de l'Académie Française, 3 vols., 4to.

————— Francais—Anglais ....*Nugent et Ouiseau.*

————— Complet, Francais, Allemand, Anglais.

Didier, O.—Madame Georges.

Du Casse, A.—Mémoires du Roi Joseph, 10 vols.

Dumas, A.—Black.

————— Fernande.

————— Georges.

————— Ingenue, 2 vols.

————— Jacques Ortis.

————— La Guerre des Femmes, 2 vols.

————— La Route de Varennes.

————— La Tulipe Noire.

————— Le Chevalier de Maison Rouge, 2 vols.

————— Le Père Gigogne, vol. i.

————— Le Père La Ruine.

————— Les Borgia.

————— Les Mariages du Père Olifus.

————— Madame de Chamblay, 2 vols.

————— A. (Fils)—Antonine.

————— Aventures de Quatre Femmes.

————— Contes et Nouvelles.

————— La Dame aux Camélias.

————— La Dame aux Perles.

————— La Vie à Vingt Ans.

————— Le Docteur Servans.

————— Le Roman d'une Femme.

Duvotenay, C.—Atlas et Itinéraire de la Suisse, 1837.

ENAULT, Etienne—Comment on Aime.

———— Louis—Hermine.

Eugenio et Virginia.

Expiation, ou Esquisse d'une Vie de Femme.

Exposition Universelle, illustrée, folio, 1867.

Eynard, Charles—Vie de Madame Krudener, 2 vols.

FABRE, F.—Mademoiselle de Malavieille.

Fénélon, F., Correspondance de, 11 vols.

———— Histoire de ma Vie, 4 vols.

———— Les Aventures de Télémaque.

———— Lettres et Opuscules de

———— Œuvres de, 22 vols.

———— Tables et Revue des Ouvrages de

Ferrière, Madame de la—Grèce, Ancienne et Moderne.

Feuillet, O.—Bellah.

———— Histoire de Sibylle.

———— La Petite Comtesse.

———— Monsieur de Camors.

———— Pauvre.

———— Roman d'un Jeune Homme pauvre.

Féval, P.—Aimée.

———— Le Capitaine Simon.

———— Les Habits Noirs, 2 vols.

———— Roger Bontemps.

Feydeau, E.—Fanny.

———— Le Mari de la Danseuse.

———— Le Secret du Bonheur, 2 vols.

———— Monsieur de Saint Bertrand.

———— Sylvie.

———— Un Début à l'Opéra.

Fiquelmont, Comte de—Lord Palmerston ; l'Angleterre, &c.

Flaubert, G.—Madame Bovary, 2 vols.

Fontaine, M. de la—Fables Choisies, 2 vols.

Fontanges, Madame de—Souvenir d'Asnières.

Foucher, P.—La Vie de Plaisir.

Frémy, A.—Journal d'une Jeune Fille.

GABORIAU, E.—Ruses d'Amour.

Garengeot, R. J. C.—Traité des Opérations de Chirurgie, 1720.

Garinet, Jules—Histoire de la Magie en France.

Gasparin, A. de—Les Tables Tournantes, 2 vols.

Gautier, T.—Jettatura, (Conte.)

Genin, F.—Les Jésuites de l'Université.

Genlis, Madame de—Le Comte de Corke, &c.

———————— Les Vœux Téméraires, 2 vols.

———————— Nouveaux Romans, 2 vols.

Girardin, E. de—Emile au hasard.

Goldsmith, O.—Le Vicaire de Wakefield, (traduction.)

Goudall, L.—L'Hermine de Village.

Gourdon, E.—Louise.

Gozlan, L.—Histoire de 130 Femmes.

————— La Dernière Sœur Grise.

————— La Folle du Logis.

————— La Famille Lambert.

————— Le Baril de Poudre d'or.

————— Le Notaire de Chantilly.

Grillet, J. H.—Les Sources Thermales de Loëche.

Guichenon, S.—La Maison Royale de Savoie, 2 vols., fo., 1788.

Guide à Carlsbad, 1842.

——— au Jardin Zoologique d'Acclimatation.

——— de Gènes, 1846.

Guizot, Mons.—Histoire de Civilization en Europe.

———————— Histoire de Richard Cromwell, 2 vols.

———————— Meditations et Études Morales.

Guldenstubbé, Baron—La Realité des Esprits.

HAMILTON, A.—Mémoires du Comte de Grammont, 1783.

Heine, H.—De Tout un Peu.

Hildebrand—La Chambre Obscure, (traduction.)

Hoffman—Contes Posthumes, (traduction.)

Hopfen, Jean—La Chanteuse Ambulante, (traduction.)

Horace, Œuvres d'

Hotel de Ville de Paris, Notice sur

Houssaye, A.—Blanche et Marguerite.

———————— Les Filles d'Eve.

———————— Mademoiselle Mariani.

Huc, Mons.—L'Empire Chinois, 2 vols.

———————— Voyage dans la Tartarie.

Hugo, V.—Le Légende des Siècles.

——— Les Contemplations, 2 vols.

——— Les Chants du Crépuscule.

——— Les Misérables, 10 vols.

—— François V.—Sonnets de Shakespeare, (traduction.)

ISCANDER, A.—Idées Révolutionaires en Russie.

JARDIN des Plantes, Promenade au, 1837.

Joliet, Ch.—Le Roman de deux Jeunes Mariés.

Jourdan, L.—Un Hermaphrodite.

Juillerat, P.—Les Deux Balcons.

Junod, L.—Histoire du Pays de Neuchatel, 1863.

Jussie, Sœur Jeanne de—Le Levain du Calvanisme.

KARR, A.—Agathe et Cécile.

——— Clovis Gosselin.

——— Contes et Nouvelles.

——— De Loin et de Près.

——— Encore les Femmes.

——— Feu Bressier.

——— Geneviève.

——— Hortense.

Q

KARR, A.—La Famille Alain.
———— La Pénélope Normande.
———— Raoul.
———— Roses Noires et Roses Bleues.
Kempis, Thomas a'—L'Imitation de Jesus Christ.
Kock, P. de—La Femme, Le Mari et L'Amant.
———— L'Homme de la Nature et L'Homme Policé.
———— Madeleine.
———— Mémoires d'une Femme de Chambre.
———— Mon Voisin Raymond.
———— Un Jeune Homme Charmant.
———— Sœur Anne.
—— Chas. P. de—L'Amant de la Lune, 10 vols.
———— L'Ane à Monsieur Martin.
———— La Baronne Blaquiskof.
———— La Famille Braillard, 2 vols.
———— Le Petit Fils de Cartouche.
———— Le Sentier aux Prunes.
———— Les Compagnons de la Truffe, 2 vols.
———— Les Demoiselles de Magasin, 2 vols.
———— Les Enfants du Boulevard.
———— Les Femmes, le Jeu, et le Vin.
———— Madame de Montflanquin, 2 vols.
———— Monsieur Choublanc.
———— Une Grappe de Groseille.
—— Henri de—Je me tuerai demain.
———— La Feé aux Amourettes.
———— La Voleuse d'Amour.
———— Le Roman d'une Femme Pale.
———— Les Mémoires d'un Cabotin.
———— Ninie Guignon.

LAMARTINE, A. de—Geneviève, Histoire d'une Servante.
———————— Jocelyn.

LAMARTINE, A. de, Œuvres de
Landelle, G. de la—Une Haine à Bord.
Lecomte, J.—Le Poignard de Cristal.
Leo, A.—Un Mariage Scandaleux.
Le Sage, A. R.—Le Diable Boiteux.
Louis Philippe d'Orleans—Mon journal des Evènements de 1815.
Lundeberg, A.—La Perle Trouvée.

MADELÈNE, J. de la—Les Ames en Peine.
Maimbourg, M.—Histoire du Calvinisme, 1612.
Maintenon, Mde. de, Lettres de, 7 vols.
——————————— Mémoires de, par De la Beaumelle, 5 vols.
Malebranche, N.—La Recherche de la Vérité, 4 vols.
Malot, H.—Les Amours de Jacques.
Mark-Bayeux, A.—Une Femme de Cœur.
Marmontel, J. F.—Contes Moraux, 3 vols., 1765.
——————— Les Incas, 2 vols.
Massillon, M.—Conférences, Discours et Sermons.
Masson, M.—Les Drames de la Conscience.
——————— Les Incendiaires, 3 vols.
Maudit, Le, par l'Abbé * * *
Menière, P.—Etudes Médicales sur les Poètes Latins.
Meray, A.—Violette.
Mery, J.—La Guerre du Nizam.
—————— Le Chateau Vert.
—————— Les Mystères d'un Chateau.
—————— Une Histoire de Famille.
Meyer, J. T.—Voyage pittoresque depuis Tyrol jusqu'à Milan.
Michaelis, S.—Histoire de Louis Gaufridi, un Magicien, &c., 1613.
Michelet, J.—La Sorcière.
Miertsching, M.—Journal de Voyage au Pole Nord.
Molière, J. B., Œuvres de, 6 vols., 4to., 1734.
————————————— 4 vols., 1750.
Monsieur X et Madame * * *

Q 2

Montaigne, M. de, Essais de, 10 vols., 1754.

Montemerli, Comtesse—Les Sensations d'une Morte.

Montolieu, Madame—Les Chateaux Suisses, 2 vols.

Muller, E.—La Driette.

Munich, Catalogue des Tableaux à, 1845.

Mürger, H.—Le Roman de toutes les Femmes.

———— Madame Olympe.

———— Les Vacances de Camille.

Musset, A. de—Contes.

NODIER, C.—Contes de la Veillée.

———— Contes Fantastiques.

———— Nouvelles.

———— Romans.

Noriac, J.—Journal d'un Flaneur.

——— La Bêtise Humaine.

——— La Dame à la Plume Noire.

——— Le Grain de Sable.

——— Mademoiselle Poucet.

——— Mémoires d'un Baiser.

OURLIAC, E.—Nouvelles.

———— Suzanne.

PALŒPHATE, Traité de, touchant les histoires incroyables.

Pascal, B., Œuvres de, 5 vols., 1779.

——— Pensées de, 2 vols.

Paul, A.—Blanche Mortimer.

——— Une Dette de Jeu.

Peat, N.—Singularitiés Humoristiques, &c., en Angleterre.

Peinture, &c., Explication des Ouvrages de, *Paris*, 1861.

Perret, P.—Histoire d'une Jolie Femme.

Petits Classiques Francois, 11 vols., viz. :—

    1 Conjuration du Comte de Fiesque, par le Cardinal de Retz.

2 Œuvres Choisies de Sarrazin.

3 La Guirlande de Julie.

4 Relation des Campagnes de Rocroi et de Fribourg.

5 Madrigaux de Monsieur de la Sablière.

6 Petites Poésies du Chevalier D'Aceilly.

7 Voyage de Chapelle et Bachaumont.

8 Œuvres Choisies de Sénecé.

9 Fables de Fénélon.

10 Poésies de Madame Evelines Désormery.

11 ———— Charles Nodier.

Platon, Dialogues de, 3 vols.

———— Les Lois.

———— L'Etat ou la Republique.

Pline—Histoire Naturelle, 12 vols., 1771.

Plutarque, Œuvres Morales de, 1613.

Polignac, Mémoires de la Duchesse de, 1796.

Pontmartin, A. de—Contes et Nouvelles.

Presbytère, Le, 2 vols.

Prévost, Abbé—Histoire de Manon Lescaut.

RABELAIS, F., Œuvres de, 3 vols., 1741.

Racine, Jean, Œuvres de, 3 vols., 1760.

Récamier, Madame, Souvenirs et Correspondance de, 2 vols.

Renan, Ernest—Etudes d'Histoire Religieuse.

———— Vie de Jésus.

Resimont, C.—Le Magnétisme Animal.

Restaut, M.—Grammaire Française, 1780.

Révélations Divines et Mystérieuses.

Reybaud, L.—Edouard Mongeron.

———— Le Coq du Clocher.

Rive, W. de la—William Haldimand.

Rivière, Jean B. de la—Sermons, avec son éloge historique, 1746.

———— H.—La Main Coupée.

Rochefoucauld, Duc de la—Maximes et Réflexions Morales.

Rossignol, L.—Lettres d'un Mauvais Jeune Homme.

Rousseau, J. J.—La Nouvelle Héloise, 4 vols., 1764.

———————— Œuvres de, 20 vols.

Ruffini, J.—Découverte de Paris par une Famille Anglaise.

SAINT-FELIX, Jules de—Les Amoureux de la Comtesse.

———————————— Les Cousines de Satan.

Saintine, B.—Picciola.

———————— Seul.

Sand, George—Antonia.

———————— Autour de la Table.

———————— Constance Verrier.

———————— Consuelo, 4 vols.

———————— Elle et Lui.

———————— François le Champi.

———————— Histoire de ma Vie.

———————— Horace.

———————— Lélia.

———————— Indiana.

———————— L'Homme de Neige, 2 vols.

———————— La Comtesse de Rudolstadt, 2 vols.

———————— La Famille de Germandre.

———————— La Mare au Diable.

———————— La Petite Fadette.

———————— La Ville Noire.

———————— Le Compagnon du Tour de France, 2 vols.

———————— Le Péché de Monsieur Antoine, 2 vols.

———————— Les Beaux Messieurs de Bois-Doré, 2 vols.

———————— Les Maitres Sonneurs.

———————— Mademoiselle de Quintinie.

———————— Marquis de Villemer.

———————— Mauprat.

———————— Mont Revêche.

———————— Nouvelles.

Sand, George—Secrétaire Intime.

———————— Tamaris.

———————— Téverino.

———————— Valentine.

———————— Valvèdre.

Sandeau, J.—Catherine.

———————— La Maison de Penarvan.

———————— Nouvelles.

———————— Sacs et Parchemins.

———————— Un Héritage.

Sardou, V.—La Perle Noire.

Scholl, A.—Les Gens Tarés.

Ségalas, Madame A.—Contes du Nouveau Palais de Cristal.

Ségur, Comte—Napoléon et la Grande Armée, 2 vols.

Serret, E.—Une Jambe de Moins.

Sevigné, Madame de—Lettres à ses filles et à ses Amis, 8 vols.

Soulié, F.—Au Jour le Jour, 4 vols.

———————— Deux Nouvelles par une Vieille Femme.

———————— Le Conseiller d'Etat.

———————— Les Deux Cadavres.

———————— Marguerite.

———————— Réalités de la Vie Domestique.

———————— Si Jeunesse Savait—Si Vieillesse Pouvait.

Souvestre, E.—Deux Misères.

———————— Confessions d'un Ouvrier.

———————— Le Mendiant de St. Roch.

———————— Sous la Tonnelle.

St. Pierre, B. de—Paul et Virginie.

Staël, Madame de—Corinne, 3 vols.

———————— De L'Allemagne, 3 vols.

———————— Révolution Française, Considérations de la

Statues de Bronze à Innsbruck, Déscription des

Streinz, W.—Les Bains de Gastein, 1831.

Sue, Eugène—Les Secrets de l'Oreiller, 4 vols.

Sue, Eugene—Le Marquis de Létorière.
———— Mystères de Paris, 6 vols.

TERRAIL, P. du—Les Galanteries de Nancy-la-Belle.
Thérésa, Mémoires de, par elle-même.
Töpffer, R.—Réflexions et Menus Propos d'un Peintre Génevois.
———— Rosa et Gertrude.
Tomlinson, L.—Astronomie Amusante, (traduction.)

UCHARD, M.—La Comtesse Diane.
———— Le Mariage de Gertrude.
———— Raymon.
———— Une Dernière Passion.
Ulbach, L.—Les Secrets du Diable.

VALREY, M.—Les Filles sans Dot.
———— Les Victimes du Mariage.
———— Marthe de Montbrun.
Vernier, V.—Comment aiment les Femmes.
Virgile—Les Géorgiques, par Delille, 1770.
Vivier, E. du--De la Mélancolie.
Voltaire, M. de—Dictionnaire Philosophique, 7 vols.
———— Théatre de, 6 vols., 1764.
Voyage autour de ma Chambre, 1817.

WEILAND, F.—Grammaire Grecque.
Weiss, Ch.—Histoires des Refugiés Protestants de France, 2 vols.
Wellenheim, L. W. de—Catalogue de Monnaies et Medailles.
Wey, F.—Dick Moon en France.

GERMAN.

Allgemeinfassliche Thierseelenkunde, 1852.
Braune, F. A. A. von—Fremden Führer nach Ischl.

Bürger, G. A.—Sämmtliche Werke.

Byron, Lord—Hebräische Gesange.

Christliche Kinderschriften.

Das Land ob der Enns (Karte).

Daumer, G. F.—Mittheilungen über Kaspar Hauser.

Deutscher Volks Kalender, 1842, 1844, 1846, 1848.

Deutsches Volksbüchlein für Jung und Alt, 1842.

Drarler, M. C.—Rheinisches Taschenbuch, 1848.

Emil * * von—Besuche in den Umgebungen Ischels.

Evangelische Kirche Deutschlands, 7 vols.

Evangelisches Gesang-Buch.

Feder, J. G. H.—Lehrbuch der Practischen Philosophie.

Feuerbach, A. von—Kaspar Hauser, der Thronerbe von Baden.

Gedichte Ludwigs des Ersten, 4 vols.

Gessner, Salomon—Schriften, 4 vols.

Goëthe, J. von—Faust.

———————— Sämmtliche Werke, 30 vols.

Grimm die Brüder—Kinder und Hausmärchen.

Heer, Dr. O.—Flora Tertiaria Helvetiæ, folio.

Humboldt, A.—Ansichten der Natur, 2 vols.

Kaiser, J. A.—Pfäfers und Hof Ragaz.

Kerner, J.—Geherin von Prevorst, 2 vols.

Kletke, H.—Almanach Deutscher Volksmährchen, 1840.

Körner, Theodore—Sämmtliche Werke.

Lieder und Gedichte.

Luther, Martin—Hauspostille, *Berlin*, 1852.

Poppel, J.—Malerische Ansichten aus Nürnberg.

————— Venedig, 24 Ansichten.

Riehl, W. H.—Naturgeschichte des Volkes, 3 vols.

Sächsische Volks Kalender für 1848.

Salzkammergut, in Ober Oesterreich (Karte).

Schiller, F. von—Geschichte des Dreissigiährigen Kriegs, 2 vols.

————— Sämmtliche Werke, 10 vols.

Volks Kalender, 1846.

ITALIAN.

Boccaccio, Giovanni—Decamerone, 4to.
Dante, A.—La Divina Commedia.
Dizionario Italiano-Francese.
Guarina, Battista—Il Pastor Fido, 1736.
Guida al Lago di Como, 1842.
Kempis, T. a'—Dell' Imitatione di Christi, 1675.
Moneti dei Paleologi.
Petrarcha, F., Le Rime di, 4to., 1711.
Ranza, Gio. A.—La Balia, Poemetto di Luigi Tansillo.

GREEK AND LATIN.

Æschylus—Agamemnon, with Annotations by F. A. Paley.
————— Prometheus Vinctus, ,, ,, ,,
Allen, J.—Synopsis Medicinæ Practicæ, 2 vols., 1729.
Analecta Veterum Poetarum Græcorum, 3 vols.
Aristotelous Peri Poiētikēs.
Attici Oratores, 16 vols.
Bartholinus, T.—Anatomia, 1651.
Bate, G.—Elenchi Motuum Nuperorum in Angliâ, 1661.
Bernard,R.—Thesaurus Biblicus seu Promptuarium Sacrum,fo.
Boerhaave, H.—Institutiones Medicæ, 1752.
Bonetus, Thomas—Anatomia Practica, 2 vols., folio, 1700.
Calendarium Inquisitionum post mortem, Hen. III. to Jas. I.
Catullus, Tibullus, Propertius, 1600.
Curtis, William—Flora Londinensis, vol. i., folio, 1777.
Dale, Samuel—Pharmacologia, 4to., 1737.
Demosthenes—Orationes Selectæ, 1731.
Diemerbrock, I.—Anatome Corporis Humani, 4to., 1683.
Donaldson, J.—Jashar; Fragmenta Carminum Hebraicorum.
Drury,H.—Arundines Cami; Eng. Poetry, trans. into Gr. & Lat.
Erasmus, D.—Colloquia Familiara, 1697.

Fabricius, H.—Pentateuchos Chirurgicum, *Francofurti*, 1733.

Freind, John—Opera Omnia Medica, folio, 1733.

Geoffroy, S. F.—Materia Medica, Tractatus de, 1741.

Graaf, R. de—Tractatus de Virorum Organis, &c.

Grosius, Heningus—Magica de Spectris, &c., 1756.

Haller, Albert—Prælectiones Academicæ, vols. ii. iv. v. vi., 1745.

Heister, Laurence—Chirurgicæ Institutiones, 4to., 1739.

Hieroclis Opera.

Homeri ,, 5 vols.

Horatii ,,

———————— illustrated by Pine, 2 vols., 1733.

Inquisitionum in Officio Rotulorum Cancellariæ Hiberniæ, 2 vols.

———————— Returnatarum Abbreviatio, 3 vols., folio.

Isocratis Scripta, *Basle*, 1587.

Juvenalis, D. Junii, Satiræ xvi.

Kempis, T. a'—De Imitatione Christi.

Landor, Savage—Poemata et Inscriptiones, 1847.

Lexicon, Græco-Latinum, 1832.

Linwood, G.—Anthologia Oxoniensis.

Nersetis Clajensis, Arminiorum Patriarchæ, Preces Sancti, 1837.

Nonarum Inquisitiones in Curia Scaccarii, temp. Edw. III., fo.

Pharmacopœia Londinensis, 1746.

Pindari Lyricorum Principis, 1616; MS. Notes by S.T.Coleridge.

Pitcairn, Archibald—Opera Omnia, 4to., 1722.

Placita de Quo Warranto, temp. Edward I.—III., folio.

Placitorum Abbreviatio, temp. Richard I.—Edward II., folio.

Platonis Opera Omnia, 8 vols.

Poetæ Minores Græci, 4 vols.

Quinctilianus, M. F.—De Institutione Oratoria, 2 vols.

Relhan, Richard—Flora Cantabrigiensis, 1785.

Rotuli Hundredorum, Henry III. and Edward I., 2 vols., folio.

—— Scotiæ, Edward I. to Henry VIII., 2 vols., folio.

Rotulorum Cancellariæ Hiberniæ Calendarium, Hen. II. to VII.

———— Originalium Abbreviatio, Hen. III. to Edw. III., fo.

Roy, H. de—Fundamentorum Medicorum, 1647.
Sabrinæ Corolla ; Renderings of English Poetry into Gr. & Lat.
Smith, James E.—Plantarium Icones, folio, 1789.
Sophocles—Tragœdiæ Septem.
Spenerus, P. J.—Insignium Theoria seu Operis Heraldici, 1717.
Taylor, Robert—Miscellanea Medica, 4to., 1761.
Valor Ecclesiasticus, temp. Henry VIII., 6 vols., folio.
Virgilius, P.—Bucolica, Georgica, et Æneis, 4to., 1757.

———

ADDENDA.

Anspach, Margravine of, Memoirs of, 2 vols.
British Catalogue of Books, 1837—1857.
Grimm, Baron de, Memoirs and Adventures of, 2 vols.
Macmillan's Magazine, 1859 to 1867, 17 vols.
Poems, &c., Miscellaneous
Rome, History of, L. C. C., 2 vols.

LEACH AND SON, STEAM PRINTERS, WISBECH.

For EU product safety concerns, contact us at Calle de José Abascal, 56–1°, 28003 Madrid, Spain or eugpsr@cambridge.org.

www.ingramcontent.com/pod-product-compliance
Ingram Content Group UK Ltd.
Pitfield, Milton Keynes, MK11 3LW, UK
UKHW040616240426
470322UK00010B/159